Two Voyages I Remember

Josh,

Reading is a voyage
you too can remember.

Cornelius "Big" Sawyer

Two Voyages I Remember

✦

A Merchant Mariner's Memoir

Cornelius "Buzz" Sawyer

iUniverse, Inc.

New York Lincoln Shanghai

Two Voyages I Remember
A Merchant Mariner's Memoir

Copyright © 2005 by Cornelius Sawyer

iUniverse books may be ordered through booksellers or by contacting:

iUniverse
2021 Pine Lake Road, Suite 100
Lincoln, NE 68512
www.iuniverse.com
1-800-Authors (1-800-288-4677)

ISBN-13: 978-0-595-36587-6 (pbk)
ISBN-13: 978-0-595-81017-8 (ebk)
ISBN-10: 0-595-36587-6 (pbk)
ISBN-10: 0-595-81017-9 (ebk)

Printed in the United States of America

Contents

Acknowledgments

Disclaimer: Some of the names and subjects in my book have been changed to protect the innocent!

Acknowledgements of Love and Support to:

Ruth Finley and Barbi Speight whose efforts made this book a reality.

Auckland, New Zealand: The Henderson Family.

Burnie, Australia: The Hefford Family, the Liotta Family, George, Sue and Nicole, and the Stewart Family.

Bayonne, New Jersey: In memory of my confessor and friend, Rev. Dominic Del Monte.

Brisbane, Australia: Friends in Carina and Hamilton.

Charleston, South Carolina: In memory of my brother McPhail Sawyer and his family, Shirley Thomas and her daughter Layontra.

Darlington, South Carolina: My sister Juanita Sawyer and sister-in-law Marie Sawyer Ruth, Cropsey Cheeseboro, Ruby, Julius and Julia.

Hobart, ~~New Zealand~~ Australia: My friends in Warrain.

Inglewood, California: Pauline Rice.

Lenox, California: James Long.

Melbourne, Australia: Trevor & Murray and their Family.

New Orleans, Louisiana: All the friends I met there who made my stay in New Orleans one of the best ever.

Norfolk, Virginia: Bernard Singleton, Lisa, Cathy, Lois, Mary Brown, Brenda, Friends at Cromwell House including Ruth, ex-sailor Alan, Lisa, Elnora, Buerlina, Curtis, Gould, Charles Weston, Rose and Ken, Danny, Papa John, Charlie, Diane, Jerry, and Chief Andy.

Olongapo, Philippines: Associates on Magsaysay Boulevard.

Portland, Oregon: Benjamin, Betsy and Karl, Big Jim, Christopher, Corina, Dustin, Geoffrey, George, Jean Marie, Keith, Kelly, Kristi, Mike, Marlene, Nick, Patricia Knight, Rob, Robb Brown, Sherryl and December, Tony, Travis and Nicole, Dick and Ken; thank you all for your encouragement.

Portsmouth, Virginia: Al Davis.

San Francisco, California: Betty, Eddy, Mattie, Norvella, and Steve.

Seattle, Washington: The Kincaid Family.

Saigon, Vietnam: My friends in Cholon and Khanh Hoi.

Sydney, Australia: The Friemanis Family, Helen and family, Irene at *Calamity Jane's*, and Jodi.

Virginia Beach, Virginia: George Davis.

And finally: the Captain, Officers, and Crew of the *S.S. Marine Charger* from 1966 to 1967.

PROLOGUE

As a child of the Great Depression, I was born in Darlington County, South Carolina in 1930, the second youngest of ten children brought up by poor, God-fearing parents of African American descent. I lived on a farm until the age of 15, three years after my father passed on. My mother found it appropriate to give up farming and move into the city because my older sisters and brothers were getting married and moving away.

By the time I finished high school, in 1947, I knew I would one day be fulfilling my dreams of traveling the world. It all started when I dropped out of college at Kentucky State in Frankfort in 1951. I joined the Navy making a world cruise in 1954.

Later in the Merchant Marines I made my first voyage to Australia and New Zealand, stopping briefly in Tahiti and Pago Pago in the late 1960's. After eight voyages to the Far East and Southeast Asia, I decided to take off from shipping and return to academia as a middle-aged student in 1971. I received a Bachelor of Art's degree in history in 1972 at San Francisco State University. I had been taking summers off from shipping to attend college there since the late 1960's. I also did post-baccalaureate studies at Portland State University in Oregon.

I have met wonderful people here in Oregon who compelled me to return again and again, staying a little longer each visit. My main reason for returning so often was to keep in touch with friends I met here in the 70's, 80's, and 90's, including a few faculty members and some workers in the maintenance department at Portland State. Several security guards at various supermarkets named Sarai and Richard were also instrumental in always making my visit enjoyable.

Several of my instructors tried to persuade me to stop going to sea and enter the field of education, but this advice fell on deaf ears, even from my friend Betty. In spite of my success in completing my education, my first love was the sea. Betty, my companion in life, understood that. What others thought didn't matter. We had our understanding. She would not go with me to Oregon or later to Long Beach, California or Norfolk, Virginia. One move from New York to San Francisco was enough for her. She became the homebody type. My friends or her friends couldn't understand what we had in common. We both knew we had our own thing going on, and I knew she would always be waiting when I returned to San Francisco.

Over the years after a number of voyages to Europe, the Middle East, Africa, South America, and the Caribbean, I came ashore briefly between shipping to try my hand at substitute teaching in the Norfolk public schools. I had bought a condominium in Norfolk's east Ocean View. I would always sub in the fall and winter at the high schools and middle schools, then returned to sea come late spring and summer. I enjoyed my experience working with these teenage students, especially after I made it clear to them that I would expect nothing from them than the same respect they gave their regular teachers. I mostly subbed language and social studies.

I retired from going to sea in 1996 after little more than 38 years sailing. I enjoyed my seasonal employment with the Norfolk public schools so much I stayed on subbing several years before returning to California and Oregon.

I found out that many of my friends in Norfolk from the 1960's had passed on. Time moved on. I saw Lucinda and Tommy as well as Brenda and Danny. My friend and fellow teacher Miss Kidd and I are still on a good friendship basis. She is still an English teacher.

As much as I enjoyed my experience working with the Norfolk public schools, I have no regrets in choosing a career at sea over a career in education. My travel experience was an education in itself. I visited parts of South Carolina occasionally since returning to the West Coast, more than five years ago, to visit with relatives and old friends.

I truly miss Norfolk: checking in with old friends on Church Street, a drive to nearby Hampton for an appointment at the nearby V.A. Medical Center, and a brief stop over on the Hampton University campus next door.

Now, I often shuttle between California and Oregon, all the while keeping in close contact with Betty.

The following is my experience as I lived and witnessed. It is true to the best of my knowledge and memory. I can pride myself in such a good recollection of events in spite of there being such a long lapse in time. From the Land Down Under to the Far East, I sincerely hope you will be able to follow me in my courses of travel.

Cornelius "Buzz" Sawyer
Portland, 2005

1

THE MARINE CHARGER

Leaving a lady friend's home in San Francisco's Sunset District in early November 1966, nostalgia again set in. It would be different now going back to sea as a civilian compared to my earlier Navy experiences. I had spoken to Betty about my plans to go sailing on a Merchant Marine ship, to Vietnam preferably and anywhere in the world as an alternative. Betty at first didn't believe me.

"What about your plan to go back to school?" she asked.

I told her or rather reminded her that I was 36 years old, been out of college 15 years, and that a little more time out wouldn't hurt. She wished me well but was dead set against my sudden decision.

I had sent away for my Seaman papers through the Coast Guard. They came back, surprisingly, less than a month later. My next move was to register with the Union. With Seaman documents in my possession and my experience on sea vessels, that would be no problem. Then, in the Port of San Francisco, maritime unions were readily available due to the escalation of the Vietnam War. Jobs were at an all-time high in the shipping halls. It was a desperate situation for shipping officials. They had to crew the many ships recently taken out of mothballs to aid in the war effort. Of course, they were looking for experienced men but eventually they were forced to take men with minimal experience.

I didn't have to do too much soul-searching. My low-paying hospital job and splitting my nephew's tuition with my sister kinda kept me financially low-keyed. Thank goodness my nephew was in his last year at a private college in North Carolina. I would go on a so-called leave of absence from my hospital job but my boss, as well as my co-workers, knew it was quits.

◆　　◆　　◆

I took off several days from my job to take a seat in the Union Hall. I didn't have to wait long. My second day in the National Maritime Union Hall the dis-

3

patcher called out a Saloon Messman job on Northern Marine Line's ship, the *S.S. Marine Charger*, destination: Australia and New Zealand. I rushed to the window to make my bid for the job. I kept saying to myself that I didn't have a chance with the hall filled with Seamen much more senior to me. A shockwave raced through my system when the dispatcher called the job for group one and there were no takers. Then he called out group two which was my category. Another shockwave engulfed me when five guys I talked with the day before, senior to me, stood back from the window in my behalf. I nervously tossed my card in the window before it went to open boards. The dispatcher and patrolman checked my credentials, mainly to see whether my Union dues were all paid up. With all that taken care of, they sent me just around the corner on California Street to pass the doctor's physical. I passed the doctor with flying colors in a "Fit for Duty" status. This early afternoon in November was one of the most exciting times of my life. My next order of business was to get to Pier 39 and on the ship. I barely had the time to pack and tell my landlady the news. Before leaving the hall I asked an old-timer how I got this job so easy. He told me the reason was that most Seamen were waiting for payoffs from ships due in port within several days. All these ships had Military contracts, back loading in San Francisco and Oakland before heading to Vietnam. Some made short refueling stops in Yokohama, Japan.

It was a clear-cut case of dollars and cents. These ships would sometimes shuttle after offloading their cargo in various Vietnamese ports. The shuttle runs may include such places as Japan and Taiwan. A return to Vietnam to offload, as well as more shuttles, would often keep them in the War Zone for maybe six months or more. The pay bonus was two-for-one in the War Zone and hauling ammunition offered another ten percent. Commercial runs to places like Australia and New Zealand or anywhere outside the War Zone offered no such incentives.

◆   ◆   ◆

I rushed to the ship grateful that it was on the San Francisco side of the Bay instead of the Oakland side. The Chief Steward, Bruce Williams, checked out my credentials. He told me that the guy I was replacing quit by mutual consent. He was a troublemaker as well as a goof-off. Bruce reminded me that my day would start at 06:30 the next morning.

◆   ◆   ◆

I was so full of excitement I had no appetite. When I took Betty out to dinner she was also excited, but not as much as I was. She ate her roast beef dinner heartily while I bird-picked mine. After leaving the restaurant we talked small talk about my landlady looking after my place. After spending the night at Betty's place she drove me to the ship on her way to her office job.

◆   ◆   ◆

The *Marine Charger* was a tramp-type steam ship going anywhere in the world necessary. She was strictly a cargo ship with refrigeration, but no air-conditioning in the sleeping quarters. Her homeport was in New York and would seldom stop on the West Coast before sailing to Asia and other ports in the South Pacific. This time coming around from New York, the Company had some emergency cargo to pick up in San Francisco.

The crew and officers would sign on at 09:00 Tuesday morning. After I finished serving breakfast Bruce reminded me to go up topside to the Purser's office to sign on for the foreign voyage. It was cloud nine all over for me. We would be setting sail for Sydney and have a brief stopover in Pago Pago for refueling early the next day.

◆   ◆   ◆

We spent only 12 hours in Pago Pago, American Samoa; sailing again before midnight. There was just enough time for wining and dining and, if you could find them, women and song. Most of the crew who went ashore patronized the hole-in-the-wall type bars near the ship. Some found a swank hotel lounge up the way among the palms. It was quite a classy place. According to some locals, Rita Hayworth filmed her movie *Miss Sadie Thompson* there in the early 1950's.

Surprisingly, beer was sold right on the dock. Some of the younger crew members took advantage of the situation. They immediately started quenching their thirst in the tropical heat. Their enjoyment was short-lived. A young dock officer approached the partying Seamen and told them that there would be no more drinking alcoholic beverages on the dock. Where there's a will, there's a way! The merrymakers complied by taking their six-packs out of view and continuing the party. So much for Pago Pago!

2

SYDNEY

The morning of November 7 we were sailing into Sydney Harbor. It was a bright, warm Thursday with sunshiny, early summer weather.

What a command view! The Harbor Bridge dominated the scenery, followed by tall and modern buildings in the background. I didn't notice the Sydney Opera House because although it was started in 1957, a change in architects meant it was not completed until 1973. Passing Circular Quay I was anxious to get into one of these pubs where I had heard that some real down-to-earth Jazz could be heard. Soon we were at Darling Harbor where the Deck Department and the Australian longshoremen were very busy tying up the ship. It had been ideal weather at sea. Sydney had been the dream port of this particular voyage. By noon we had cleared both customs and immigration.

◆　　◆　　◆

My co-worker Charlie and I finished serving lunch promptly at 12:30. He went right away to our quarters for a nap. We would be off for three hours but I felt too excited to sleep. Instead I went a short distance to George Street to shop at Woolworth's and then on to a nearby chocolate store. In my opinion, Australia has some of the best chocolate in the world. Well worth forgoing a nap for. I learned other crewmen thought likewise. By 18:30 Charlie and I had finished serving dinner to the officers, cleaned up, and were in a taxi on our way to King's Cross, better known as "the Cross."

This was by far the most popular meeting place in Sydney for Seamen from the ships, tourists, and the American Military on rest and relaxation from Vietnam. Most people who came to Sydney from elsewhere would make the Cross a must-see before leaving town and the crew of the *Marine Charger* was no exception.

◆   ◆   ◆

You could find just about anything you wanted and some things you might not want at the Cross. My best advice was, "When available, take what you want; and what you don't want, leave alone."

We got out of a taxi and entered *The Greenroom*, a pub where Charlie's lady friend was waiting for him. Charlie had been to Australia before on other ships. At 68 years old he still managed to attract young women, some of them barely in their twenties. His manner of dress played a part. He dressed immaculately, always wearing expensive suits and ties ashore although he was only a Saloon Messman like me. He would often receive compliments on the way he dressed from other shipmates, including the Captain and Chief Mate. We worked together and sometimes went ashore together. I often wore casual sports clothes. I felt humble in his presence. We were a generation apart in age but hit it off right away. I admired his commonsense know-how. He only had an elementary school education while I, at 36, had a little better than a year to go on a college degree. We sometimes goofed around onboard and ashore when put to simple tasks. So brothers we were. Once in *The Greenroom* Charlie's lady friend spotted him right away.

"Charlie!" she screamed.

After they finished embracing and kissing, he handed a gift to her which was some expensive perfume.

Then he introduced us, "Buzz, Alice. Alice, Buzz."

"My pleasure," I said after his introduction.

"Likewise," she responded in her polished Australian accent.

The evening was young and I knew they had quite a bit of unfinished business to take care of. I decided to excuse myself and checkout some more of the happenings in *The Greenroom*. There was plenty to do my first night ashore. I made it a point not to get too wasted. After all I had the whole weekend ahead of me. I went to the bar and ordered a rum and Coke. I knew right away I was drinking on foreign turf because the drink tasted weaker than those in any American bar I had patronized. I knew then I would switch to beer preferably Foster's, which is much stronger in alcohol content than American Budweiser. *The Greenroom* was becoming more crowded as the evening wore on. The people streaming in were mostly young, from all walks of life. A few were leaving to go on a "pub crawl," the Australian slang for barhopping. More people were coming in than were leaving. Some of the customers were soldiers and sailors both Australian and American. A few came in wolf packs, but most of them came escorting lovely young ladies. Some members of the crowd were ordinary working people: office girls, telephone operators, hotel workers, and foodservice workers out on a Thursday night starting their weekend early. Some were even hustlers and streetwalkers. The crowd also included men who were longshoremen, hotel workers, cooks, waiters, and yes, even a drag queen who dropped in from a pub down the street called *Les Femmes.*

I observed that these people of various backgrounds got along well. There was not one scuffle or fight the whole evening. Three young bouncers were on duty for good measure. One of them was a Maori, or native of New Zealand; the other two were White. They did a good job of keeping the peace by moving among the crowd and observing every detail.

The drag queen I mentioned earlier went by the name of Katrina. One of the girls at the bar spoke of her as being a professional entertainer at *Les Femmes.* Apparently Katrina was well known in the Cross. Many of the dudes, including some with ladies, yelled her name as she walked in the door. She received a few hugs along the way. Before she could order at the bar she had three Napoleon brandies in front of her. She chatted briefly with people who had surrounded her while nonchalantly sipping Napoleons which had grown in number.

◆ ◆ ◆

Twenty minutes later Katrina walked out of the door with body guards in tow. She had to be on stage at *Les Femmes* within the hour. Seeing Katrina in that white and black lace gown, make up, and long blonde hair, I could not imagine her being anything but a she, and I was ready to call anyone who said otherwise the biggest liar in Sydney.

Les Femmes is a good example of the surprising tolerance of gays in Australia, at least in the larger cities. It takes in large crowds who pay dearly to get laughs and give applause to the guys who put on knock out shows. These entertainers get paid huge salaries for their services. But mind you all Australians are not so liberal when it comes to gays. Some display outright hatred, calling them "puftas" and "camps." Sometimes Australians go on "queer bashing" sprees. In larger cities like Sydney, Melbourne, and Brisbane it happens less often. In rare cases some gay men have been shot, especially in the Outback which is a cultural world removed from Sydney.

◆   ◆   ◆

The Greenroom kept its party type atmosphere on into the wee hours. Guys from the ship kept dropping in; some with girls, others in search of girls. The Chief Cook Kevin O'Keefe, known to his shipmates as "K.O.," and the two young Messmen came in and took seats at a corner table. Dale and Jake were looking all eagle eyed at the excitement while K.O. remained nonchalant. His mind was clearly back in Saigon. Within five minutes three girls they had asked to join them, happily obliged. Jake and Dale could not believe their luck. Jesse, the Second Cook, came in and immediately spotted a girl he hadn't seen in several years. He hadn't gotten into his drunken mood just yet, so they started renewing old acquaintances. Within ten minutes they were on their way out the door for a pleasant evening.

By this time about all of my shipmates who came to *The Greenroom* were either making out or getting some good promises. So what was I waiting for?

"Let's be sociable," I said to myself.

While sitting at the bar I noticed a very attractive, dark-complexioned young lady. She was talking to the barmaid at the center of the bar. It was obvious they knew each other. Then the bar really got busy. Their conversation was broken up by an impatient Australian wharfy anxious to quench his thirst.

I immediately took advantage of the situation in order to meet the young lady. Several questions raced through my mind. Was she alone? What would bring a Soul sister to Sydney? I was in for a very big surprise.

"I'm Sawyer, just call me Buzz," I said.

"Judy," she said extending her right hand.

"What brought you to Sydney?" I asked. I followed with another nosy question, "What part of the States are you from?"

A charming smile flashed across her face.

"States? Don't I wish!" she replied.

Right away I realized my faux pas. The minute she spoke I knew she was a local resident. She spoke in a sweet accent; a real charming lady.

Judy had never been to the States, but said she would one day love to go, especially to California or Florida. I told her I was born in South Carolina, but was presently residing in San Francisco. With a light giggle she told me how my accent stood out. I told her how my job on American ships took me around the world. Before I could ask her occupation, she said that she worked for the telephone company. She had come to Sydney from New Zealand almost ten years earlier with her parents, while still in her early teens. Her ethnic background, as I guessed, was Maori. I ordered myself another rum and Coke. She accepted a non-alcoholic drink because in a few hours she would be on her way to work. Judy really impressed me. She didn't try to lead me on. We talked small talk for nearly another hour. By that time it was the wee hours of the morning and she explained to me that she had to be on her way home. I offered to see her home, but she politely declined saying she had a ride with friends, but could meet me at *The Greenroom* Saturday night at 7:00 PM. I asked about the next night, Friday, but on that night she would be attending a concert with friends from her job. She invited me to come along, but I declined. I mainly wanted to explore some other neighborhoods in Sydney other than the Cross.

Before parting company just after midnight, I told Judy about being invited to a dance in Bankstown on Saturday night by a longshoreman on the Darling Harbor docks. I wanted her to go along as my guest. Of course that surprised her. I had only been in Sydney two days and already I was getting an invitation to a dance. After a brief hesitation, she accepted my invitation and with a smile on her face she reminded me that I wasn't wasting any time getting into the action.

"Make hay while the sun shines," I said. Judy agreed.

◆   ◆   ◆

After bidding her goodnight I went out into the night and straight into a taxi heading to the ship. I went to bed immediately. I bet my roommate Charlie was also in bed by now, at Alice's house that is, not missing a trick. I had no worry he would be late coming back to the ship to cover his job. If not I would cover both jobs with no sweat. I was feeling a bit light headed but was still in good shape the next morning when the AB, or Able-Bodied Seaman, knocked on our door yelling, "06:00!" Ten minutes later Charlie walked in looking haggard, but still fit.

After a quick clean up, we were both on the job setting up for breakfast. We would have an easy breakfast because the twelve officers we served three times a day would be fewer in numbers. At least five or six of them would still be at their girlfriends' homes. Even the crew, who were on duty would get a standby and be off part of the day. After all, this was Sydney.

All of the Steward Department was on station and working. Jesse, though hung-over, was fixing breakfast while talking about the good time he had last night with his girl, Janney. Ken, the Galley Man, sat in the corner of the Galley peeling potatoes. He also talked about his night on the town, but a little more low-keyed. He talked about his wife back in Tennessee, a good woman, but he would hate to think about what would have happened if she had caught him with Deirdre last night.

K.O. said, "You would've run like hell!"

Everybody laughed including Juan, the Third Cook, who usually stayed aloof from idle gossip in the Galley.

The two young Messmen, Dale and Jake, got so carried away with Sydney that they vowed to come back and stay for a few months. That's not uncommon for young bloods that have never been overseas. Eventually they would come down from cloud nine and see both the forest and the trees.

Sydney really had its effect on the *Marine Charger's* crew, especially those who had never been there before. As for the girls, we were all smitten by the hospitality and easy pick ups. Not all pick ups were streetwalkers. Some were respectable ladies with jobs and other legitimate responsibilities. Yes, some of them did carry their American boyfriends to some dingy hotel room or back street rooming house. Many of them took their companions to swank apartments they shared with other people. And believe it or not some were still living with their parents and brought their guests home without disturbing mom or dad. No lie. All of these experiences were the talk of the ship Friday morning. Even Larry the Bedroom Steward (or BR), joined in the conversation.

Larry was sipping tea, telling about a girl he met who proposed marriage to him. Of course he politely declined. With a wife back in New York I can see why. Larry came to the States ten years earlier from a banana port in Jamaica called Port Antoine. In spite of his many years in the country he kept his clipped Jamaican accent intact.

That day we whisked through breakfast, lunch and dinner. The Deck Department really shook a leg as did the Engine Department. Most everybody was out to repeat their performances from the night before.

◆   ◆   ◆

By 18:30 I was walking into the Seamen's Club. I stayed only long enough to mail several letters to the States. One of them was to Betty back in San Francisco and the others to relatives in South Carolina. I took a stroll to the Cross by way of Garden Island where the Australian Fleet is located. I passed Garden Island to find myself right in the middle of Woolloomooloo, with its pubs, bistros, restaurants, and hotels galore. Woolloomooloo is an Aboriginal term which means "welcome to the party." And a party it was! I formed an opinion that it was just an extension of the Cross. They were in walking distance from each other and the only difference I saw was that Woolloomooloo was a bit more down to earth.

I didn't get carried away drinking because my dance and date appointment were the next night. I spent several hours pub crawling in the area before catching a taxi to a nice neighborhood called Paddington. After rubbing shoulders with some of the elite, I felt ready to head for Circular Quay. I decided to wait until another time to go out to Bondi Beach. I had no desire to stroll on a beach at night.

◆   ◆   ◆

It was party time in Circular Quay. After finding a club with music I liked, I would go no farther I had found blonde and blue-eyed Soul. This hit me like a ton of bricks. I came on this voyage to Australia with mixed emotions. The White Australia Policy was still very much in practice in 1966 barring Africans and Orientals from immigrating into the country. They made exceptions for those with special skills or who were married to an Australian. Now here I was in a bar where, other than myself, there was not a Black face in sight.

The bar was full of people applauding and screaming to Blues and Jazz. Several couples squeezed in insisting that I share their table. The imitators on stage sounded just as real as the originals. Especially the pleasantly plump young lady singing one of Billie Holiday's old songs entitled "Good Morning Heartache."

"Girl, I hear you! Wail on!" I shouted.

The couples at my table smirked then let out some light giggles. After several more Blues numbers the singer retreated from the stage followed by what seemed like never ending applause. I couldn't believe my eyes or my ears. The band played two more Jazz numbers before intermission. They were very much together. Another young female vocalist came out after intermission and sang one of Dinah Washington's numbers, "Back Water Blues."

Applause and more applause went to the drummer, who was about 60 years old, who came out at the end of the next session. I would think that those male Jazz musicians and lovely female Blues vocalists would have gotten a whole hearted nod of approval from the late Greats.

◆   ◆   ◆

After mingling briefly with some of the friendly faces inside, I found myself walking outside. I got a firm handshake from the bouncer, asking me to come again. As I climbed into a taxi, I could see the big Harbor Bridge almost directly above me. It was all lit up with heavy Friday night traffic. What a sight to behold! I first thought I wanted to go across that big bridge and check out the sights of north Sydney then come across town and cross another bridge to Pierremont and Balmain. My second thought won out, however. I asked the taxi to take me back to the ship.

◆   ◆   ◆

The next morning I was up bright and early to complete my work schedule in due time. I had consumed only three Foster's beers at eight percent if I remember right. I felt like I had guzzled a few more. I wanted to make sure nothing would interfere with my Saturday night dance and date. The day was routine with shipmates swapping sea stories of their experiences. Most of them had returned to the Cross. I hit the jackpot when I told them about my visit to the Blues and Jazz pub in Circular Quay.

"You got to be kidding!" said Bob Harris, the Bos'n, who had stopped his bacon and eggs breakfast to get an earful.

"In this White man's country?" questioned Jesse.

I told them just where to go if they doubted me. Some said they would check it out, with girlfriends in tow, that Saturday night.

"See you there," some of them said.

"No you won't," I shot back. "I have other plans tonight way out in suburbia."

I went back in the Saloon Mess to take Sully's order. As Chief Mate, he was about always on the run. He was never in the Mess Hall longer than ten minutes except when talking to the Captain about ship matters during lunch or dinner. He was a likeable old guy at 72, never any trouble to serve.

There were only seven officers in for breakfast. The Radio Operator was off duty in port. The Purser, or Paymaster, might be someplace in Sydney getting polluted, with or without female companionship. More power to all the absentees. I would see them again two days later at sea. Sea watches had been broken two days earlier so the watch standers were all on eight hour shifts instead of four, as at sea.

At lunchtime I ordered a New England boiled dinner plate from K.O. for myself. I hurriedly devoured it before the meal started at 11:30. Charlie came in, finishing up the left over dirty dishes. He told me to take my time eating, he would cover until I finished.

"Man, take it easy. That woman'll be right there tonight when you get to the Cross."

"So will Alice," I laughed back.

"She damn sure better be," he replied.

We both grabbed an apple jack among the many Juan had fixed for dessert, washing it down with a glass of fruit punch.

I served dinner but skipped the chili beans and rice for myself. This is usually on the dinner menu on Saturday along with three other entrees. I knew there would be food galore at the dance.

◆   ◆   ◆

By 18:30 I was all cleaned up. I was in a taxi on my way to the Cross along with Jesse and Charlie. As usual Charlie was immaculately dressed in an expensive, dark gray suit. Jesse was also looking decent in a gray silk mohair suit he bought in Yokohama several years earlier. As for me I was dressed in a dark blue suit I bought from Roos Atkins, a swank department store on San Francisco's Market Street. I almost forgot to pack it before sailing. All three of us were dressed in white shirts and dark blue ties. Charlie and Jesse wore Stacy Adams maroon colored shoes. I contented myself to wear a pair of black Nunn Bushes. Please pardon me if I sound braggadocios, but we were clean when we walked into *The Greenroom*. All three girls were waiting.

"Don't you look lovely," I told Judy.

She was all decked out in her after-five black party dress. She returned the compliment by saying, "Don't you look handsome. I bet you didn't buy that suit from here."

"No," I said.

I formally introduced Judy to Charlie and Jesse. Although the three girls had never met, they had seen each other at various times in *The Greenroom* and other places in the Cross and Woolloomooloo. I insisted that all six of us have a round on me. After all, Judy and I had two hours before we would show up in Bankstown. The party was on. I told Judy we would take a taxi to the dance. She would not hear a word of it. Instead, she said we would get a taxi to the station then grab a train to Bankstown. It was a fairly long ride of maybe 30 to 45 minutes. We bade goodnight to Charlie, Jesse, and their lady friends. They all wished us a good evening at the dance.

◆   ◆   ◆

On the train I noticed the names of the suburban communities. Some had names like you'd have in the States, like Willoughby, while others had odd sounding names, like Erskineville and Narwee. Judy and I chatted a bit and before long we were getting off the train and into a taxi. Gunther, the man who invited me, had given me good instructions on how to reach the dance hall. The taxi was also helpful.

We walked into the hall hand in hand. I wondered whether I should have accepted this invitation from my new-found friend, Gunther. I wasn't, or rather we weren't, about to back out. Let the chips fall where they may. Finally I spotted Gunther and Mai his wife. They immediately waved us to their table. The hall was filling up. The crowd around us at first fell silent, but after a while continued their pleasant chatter, although they could not keep their eyes off Judy and me.

Most of the guests were immigrants from the Baltic Republics of Latvia, Lithuania, and Estonia. Gunther introduced me to his wife Mai. I in turn introduced Judy to both of them and later to other guests at the table. I was happy to have met Judy two nights earlier. She was by no means a tramp or streetwalker. She could hold her own in the best of company. The attention we got was overwhelming. They wanted to know what part of America we were from.

"You go first," I whispered in her ear.

She shrugged and said, "I've never been to America or anywhere else outside of Australia and New Zealand, but maybe I'll get there one of these days."

Her Maori and Australian accent defined her clearly as being on local turf, like it or not.

Then it was my turn to answer a barrage of questions, as though I was holding a press conference. I decided to beat them to the punch by answering questions before they were asked.

"Yes, I'm from America," I volunteered. "I was born in South Carolina but have spent all my adult years in New York and on the West Coast. No, I'm not a singer or a dancer."

"Then what kind of an entertainer are you?" an old man from the other end of the table asked.

"I'm not," I answered. I was not off the hook yet.

"Do you box?" a younger man at the next table asked.

"Not really," I replied, "unless you try to back me into a corner."

"Then what brought you to Australia?" his wife asked.

"A cargo ship docked in Darling Harbor," I answered.

Then laughs and snickers came from both tables.

Gunther rescued me from this unofficial press conference by telling people at both tables that I was a friend of his. He added that we had met on the ship and he had invited me to the dance.

"Welcome!" they exclaimed almost in unison.

Curious stares turned to smiling, friendly faces. Some of them told me about their own visits to the States. Most of them had immigrated to Australia with their parents shortly after World War II. Although they had been living in Australia for a number of years, their English was heavily accented. The same pattern prevailed in the States. Gunther and Mai had visited the sights of New York and friends and relatives in Oregon five years earlier.

"I wish my parents had immigrated to America instead of Australia," Gunther said.

He said he noticed that Latvians living in the States seem to be better off than those living in Australia.

As the evening wore on the people hosting the party came over to check on us, to see if we were alright. We assured them we were never better. Several long tables in the center were laden with food and drink. I apologized to Judy for the disruption of our conversation earlier.

"No big deal," she said.

"You certainly know how to carry yourself."

I could tell she was enjoying herself. This occasion was something different for her. She seemed to never stop smiling. Gunther leaned over and whispered, asking where I met Judy. I told him that I met her at the Post Office. I didn't dare tell him I picked her up at a pub in the Cross.

The local band provided fairly good entertainment in song and play. They played a number of oldies but very few modern songs. Judy and I decided to sit out the polkas and waltzes. Then they played a twist number from the early 60's. Judy and I immediately went to the dance floor.

The vast majority of the older guests sat out the twist number, but laughed and applauded us on. Then some young couples joined us on the dance floor, making me feel a bit more comfortable. Several numbers later we returned to the floor to the tune of another early 60's song, "Moon River." On the dance floor we embraced as I gave her first a peck on the cheek and then on the lips. We danced slowly to the tune of the band in a warm embrace. She let me know in no uncertain terms how much she was enjoying herself. When we returned to the table I got up enough nerve to briefly excuse myself from Judy to approach an attractive older lady at the next table for a dance. She had been giving friendly smiles at us on and off all evening. She gladly accepted. She was a good swing dancer by the name of Helen. Gunther danced with Judy and went back on the floor once more to dance with Mai.

After checking to see what we wanted, the caterers brought food to the table for us. Refills of drinks were also in the making. It had been many moons since I received such carte blanche treatment. One faux pas on my part, after eating I should have had the common sense Judy showed. She switched from alcoholic to non-alcoholic drinks. I didn't. Although I was still in control of myself, toward the end of the dance I was feeling it. I thanked all of the guests at the table for the hospitality shown us all evening. If there were any hopes of getting to work the next morning on time, I would have to make a speedy exit by taxi, see Judy home then get back to the ship. With Sunday morning fast approaching, there would be no fooling around with trains. Gunther and Mai lived in Revesby, the next community. A couple sitting directly across from us then volunteered to drive Judy and me home. Judy lived only a short distance from the Cross. They would go that way to their home. Gunther was quite happy things were working out so well and so was Mai. They invited me to their home in Revesby but time would not allow it since the ship would be sailing early Monday. It was kind of them to extend me that visit but it would be 11 years before I would return to Sydney and accept their invitation.

◆   ◆   ◆

It was a long way back to Judy's place, but the ride seemed short. On the way, the middle-aged couple chatted in Latvian, then back to English when they spoke with us. Both husband and wife told us they looked forward to one day seeing us again. The husband was very much in command of his driving when they dropped us off at Judy's place. He seemed to have been insulted when I reached in my pocket to offer them a tip for gas, or petrol as they call it.

"Hell no!" was the answer.

Judy and I thanked them again.

"Anytime," they answered, as they drove away.

Then we went inside her cozy and neat two bedroom apartment. Oh yes! I had already invited myself to spend the night or what was left of it.

"What if you are one of those Yank prowlers?" she jokingly asked.

With a laugh I answered her I wasn't. She told me the evening out with me was one of the best she'd had in a long time.

"Likewise," I said, as we embraced and kissed.

We were not disturbing anybody. Her roommate, another Maori girl, had not yet come in from the Cross. I was feeling no pain. The alcohol was carrying on more so with me than with her. We got to bed and were partying so much I forgot to remind myself that my work day would be starting at 6:30 AM. We had a ball. Judy was everything I dreamed she would be, if not a little more. The next morning after the encore I realized my foolish mistake.

"I thought you would be off today," Judy gasped.

"Don't I wish!"

I ran to the bathroom and, after she threw me a towel, cleaned up. Her perfumed soap was really a knock out. In what seemed to be seconds I was walking out of the door. Judy had already hailed my taxi. I told her I would be about a half hour late, and would get a good chewing out from the Chief Steward.

"I'm sorry," she said.

"No big deal," I replied.

I knew Charlie would have everything covered. After a quick kiss I got in the taxi telling her I would see her at 7:00 PM or maybe a little before. I tried to shove some Australian dollars in her hand but she refused.

"Later," she said.

The young Australian taxi driver knew I was late for work so he skirted some traffic getting me there a few minutes earlier. To show my gratitude I paid him a double fare.

As I got out of his taxi he showed a broad grin saying in his strong Australian accent, "Thank you, mate. Good 'ay."

I hurried up the gangway and into the Saloon Mess and what I thought would happen, did happen. The Chief Steward was there waiting. Breakfast was about half over. There were only two officers in the Officer's Mess. Charlie had taken care of everything. He came out of the Galley with Sully's order of scrambled eggs, ham, and hash brown potatoes, and politely set it in front of him. Sully had already made his own wheat toast, as he so often did.

"Good morning my fellow shipmates," I said trying to make it look like nothing had happened.

"Is that all you have to say?" the Chief Steward barked back.

"Sorry I'm late, but we can talk after breakfast," I shot right back.

"No, we'll talk now. Step in my office," he said in a lowered tone of voice.

I complied like an obedient second grader getting chewed out as I expected. He went on to remind me that I was not on my personal yacht where I could come and go as I please. He further reminded me that I signed on to do a job. I was expected to cover my job which included being on time and not taking off during working hours without permission. As a final warning he said if I continued such acts of misbehavior my name would be placed in the log book by the Captain resulting in a dismissal from the vessel at the end of the voyage. He also reminded me of my college background, and that I should get my act together. Really I wanted to come right back at him for talking to me as though I was some child, but I knew damn well that I had been caught wrong, and that he was in charge. I gave him an affirmative nod and walked out of his office and back to work.

Now I'll tell you a few words about the Chief Steward, Bruce Williams. He was one of the best Stewards you could work for, but he was a no nonsense type of person. He would go to bat for the men in his department as long as they never forgot two things: cover their jobs and that he was in charge. Rightfully so, he could demand such respect. He had come up through the ranks in the nearly 30 years since he went to sea. He went from Messman to Third Cook, then Second Cook, Chief Cook then finally rose to the height of his ambition as Chief Steward. Over the years he bought a home for himself and family in New Jersey as well as a home for his mother in Texas. He also sent both a son and a daughter to college. As a Black, mid-fifties person, Bruce had the attitude that if he can do it as a less educated person, you can do it as a more educated person. There was never another misunderstanding between us. I had come on the ship to work and get myself ahead. I vowed to never mix business with pleasure again.

After Charlie and I finished serving breakfast and cleaning the Officer's Mess and pantry it was about 09:15, little more than an hour of free time. No nap until after lunch. Instead I went in the Galley to lend a helping hand to Ken who was peeling potatoes, carrots, and onions. His red hair seemed to be about to catch on fire. I started on the carrots since he was about finished with the onions and potatoes. Within 30 minutes we had finished.

"Thank you 'much, Buzz," he said in his Tennessee drawl.

He then went on doing other chores in the Galley for the cooks. I went out on deck to take in the sights of the Sydney skyline. There was quite a bit of activity in the harbor on this warm Sunday morning with a hot Australian summer fast approaching. Longshoremen were busy as bees loading the cargo. Gang Bosses were leaving no stones unturned, assuring us that nothing would prevent us from sailing the next day.

Lunch went across without incident. As expected, there were few customers. After serving lunch I caught a much needed two hour nap, then a mad rush through dinner. In spite of sirloin steak night there were still few takers. Sydney would win out. A few crew members brought their girlfriends aboard as visitors for several hours. They fixed them a plate of steak, baked potato, and broccoli and whisked it to their rooms or to the Recreation Room.

◆   ◆   ◆

In the Steward Department it was all ashore by 19:00. We shared a taxi to the Cross then split up to have one last fling in Sydney. Judy, her roommate Heather, and her roommate's boyfriend George were waiting at her apartment. Heather and George were going to a show but Judy insisted they wait until after my arrival. She wanted them to meet me so the show would have to wait. I was delighted to meet George, a well mannered Australian dude and Heather, who was another Maori. Almost immediately we were sitting down to dinner which came as a surprise to me. After all, 7:00 PM is a bit late for tea even for Aussies. Judy prepared Wellington stew, a large salad, dinner rolls, and of course hot tea. The four of us had a ball at the table.

"Well, my compliments to the Chef," I said.

"Thank you," said Judy.

Heather told me how Judy had bragged about our good time at the dance the night before.

"Wish we could have made that one," George volunteered.

I told them that attending that dance and meeting the three of them would be the highlight of my Australian visit.

"Thank you," they all answered together.

I dared not tell them about the chewing out I got from my boss on the ship earlier that day.

"Let sleeping dogs lie," I said to myself.

At the end of dinner Heather excused herself from the table, went to the refrigerator, and brought back a bottle of dinner wine. She filled all four glasses before rejoining us at the table.

Heather raised her glass and said, "A toast to our American friend who has graced our home with his charming presence."

Her remarks overcame me. I only managed to muster up the words, "Thank you, the honor is all mine."

Judy and I kissed as did George and Heather. Several minutes later they were on their way to the theater. I told them to enjoy the show as they walked out of the door. As Judy scraped and washed the dishes I offered to lend a helping hand, but she would not hear a word of it. I retreated to the living room to watch television while she finished cleaning the kitchen which didn't take long. It was only 8:00 PM when she joined me in the living room. Then we kind of relived our experience at the dance the night before. She had never experienced anything like it since she came to Australia. She believed she only experienced it then because she went as my guest. We went on to talk about the Civil Rights struggle in the States. She had followed it closely. I told her that I believe in integration but only to a certain extent, like economical fairness, political opportunities, and social integration, like last night. My trips around the world to meet and mingle with people of other cultures are good examples of this. But when it came to family values and the institution of marriage I chose to stay with my own.

As Booker T. Washington said, "Remain as separate as the fingers on the hand."

Then I told Judy about how I admired the Maori and other Polynesians who managed to hold on to their cultural heritage in spite of the race mixing in places like New Zealand, Tahiti, and other Polynesian habitats. She was surprised to know I had that much knowledge of her people. She smiled as she reminded me that my race also had a culture that was lost when our ancestors were uprooted out of Africa and brought to America as slaves. When freedom came over two hundred years later, the culture was lost. For a lady in her mid-twenties with only a high school education and a crash course in business administration Judy was quite versed in world affairs. We complimented each other.

Two hours had passed us by. She told me that Heather and George worked at the same restaurant in the Cross right off Darlinghurst, she as a floor person and he as a cook. It made me feel good that neither of them were street hustlers. All were just working people earning their keep. She went on to tell me that I was only enjoying Australia because I was visiting the country and didn't live there. I truthfully told her I hadn't encountered any discrimination so far.

"I doubt you will," she said.

She went on to say that I was a foreigner in a tourist status, spending money and having a damn good time.

"Racism is here. But sometimes you can't touch it like those of us who live here."

Then I asked about the Aborigines. I hadn't seen any. Not yet anyway. She said a few were around, but they were not allowed in some of the places that I patronized. What a mind blower that was! I decided not to bombard her with any further questions on race relations. Judging by what was going on in the States in late 1966 the pot had no right calling the kettle black.

We got in bed just before midnight. I was going to make sure I didn't incur the wrath of the Chief Steward this time. I only drank the dinner wine and a beer from the refrigerator so I would be sober the next morning when starting my day. Judy was up at 5:00 AM fixing lamb chops over hard eggs, fried potatoes, and, oh yes, muffins. How honored I felt! She joined me at the table after I had cleaned up. What a tasty breakfast. She drank tea, hot of course and I stuck to orange juice. We engaged in pleasant conversation during breakfast. She said she wouldn't go back to bed since she had to dress and get to work in two hours. Things were going like clockwork. After breakfast she hailed my taxi. The taxi was there in less than ten minutes. I reached in my pocket and brought out two 20 dollar bills.

"What's that for?" she asked with a startled look on her face.

"For taking such good care of me," I said.

I had to force the money in her hand. I told her groceries were a little cheaper here than in the States. Since I had eaten a bit of her groceries I told her it was time for replenishment.

"Thank you," she said as she walked me out of the door, down the steps and into the street where the taxi was waiting.

We embraced, kissed, and promised to stay in touch. I got in the taxi waving back to her. She blew me a kiss. What a beautiful sight she was with her powder blue house dress gleaming in the Australian summer morning breeze. She kept waving until we turned the corner out of sight. Judy and I did stay in touch for a long time, but it would be 11 years before we would meet again.

The taxi driver wanted to know if I enjoyed myself in Sydney. I assured him that I did. I told him about things I did and places I went in just four short days. He was really impressed. After I got out of his taxi, leaving him a handsome tip, he thanked me and invited me to come again.

3

MELBOURNE

Back aboard ship Charlie and I went through breakfast without a hitch. The Chief Steward was sitting with K.O., the Chief Cook, in the Crew Mess discussing some changes he had made on the menu for two days later. Dale and Jake the two young Crew Messmen, were cleaning the tables since the meal was about over.

"Hello Buzz," Jake said. "That was a lovely girl you were with the other night. What's she doing in Australia?"

"Thank you," I said. "She lives here."

He and his working partner mistook Judy for an American Soul sister. I didn't bother to explain the situation not then anyway. I just dismissed it as the naiveté of two young White dudes. The Steward looked up smiling.

"You enjoyed yourself I see."

"Oh, yes," came the answer.

I could tell from the look on his face that he was not that happy that I enjoyed myself, but more that I was not a bad apple in his barrel two mornings in a row.

Jesse was all hungover, but very much on top of his job. Juan was telling Ken about some additional stores he would need. Larry the BR was by now up topside taking care of the officers' cabins. Most of the Steward Department would have breakfast in the Crew Mess after the officers' ate theirs. The same policy followed dinner. Lunch was usually taken on the run, especially at sea.

I decided to go out on deck after breakfast to get one more glimpse of Sydney's skyline. My timing couldn't have been better. The cargo was all loaded and the longshoremen were on dock getting ready to cast off. I spotted Gunther and yelled down the gangway. I thanked him again for the enjoyable Saturday night get together at the dance. We bid each other farewell, but kept in touch over the years. The Deck Department was busy handling lines. Bob Harris, the Bos'n, was yelling at one of the Ordinary Seamen he had caught goofing off. We would be sailing in little less than an hour so all the crew and officers were back onboard.

Sea watches had been set at midnight for both the Engine and Deck Departments.

There was so much activity out on deck I decided it was best I get out of both the working men's way and out of harm's way. My break was almost over. I slowly walked back inside resigning myself to sail away from Sydney, New South Wales and sail north to Melbourne, Victoria.

The time at sea and the six hundred mile distance gave us time to regroup and get a second wind. Bruce asked if we in the Steward Department wanted to work an extra two hours straightening up several storerooms. We all agreed. I personally wanted to make some money back after the party spree in Sydney. We started shortly after dinner and were done and in bed by 22:00.

The next morning at 10:30, there was a fire and boat drill. The hoses were brought out, turned on and off, but the boats were not touched. A muster report was taken by the Second Mate and one of the Third Mates. Sully told the crew to answer up and tell what their duties were. Through all this, Captain Schraeder was looking down stoically from the Bridge. He didn't miss a trick. After the short fire and boat drill, I rushed back to the Officer's Mess to set up for lunch which would begin in a half hour. Lunch and dinner went by without incident. I was caught up on my naps. It was smooth sailing on into Melbourne.

Melbourne was quite a different experience than Sydney. In Sydney, the ship was docked in walking distance from downtown and many of the exciting places. You could compromise. Take a casual stroll to the action spots and later that night or early next morning take a taxi back to the ship. Not so in Melbourne. Most of the dock locations were far out. Since our stay in Melbourne was only two days some of the crew decided to stay aboard rather than suffer the inconvenience of getting to town.

The first day in port I talked with some dock workers about a few places to go in a low-keyed way, like going to a quiet pub or to a restaurant to have pizza. After all I was not quite into my second wind from the four really exciting days in Sydney. The dock worker told me about the movie houses on Bourke Street, but I hardly wanted to see a movie with just two days in town. I took note of various places they told me about so that come 19:00 I would be ready to roll. Just before dinner Bruce, Jesse, and Charlie said they wanted to go along with me to downtown Melbourne. They offered to share the taxi fare, but I told them no big thing. Then I told them about the places the dockworkers told me about. Unlike me they had been to Melbourne a few times before and did not expect it to be the likes of Sydney. We all decided to eat dinner ashore. We got pizza at an Italian restaurant. They reminded me to at least dress in a coat and tie, not necessarily in a dress suit. They reminded me because they all knew how casual I liked to dress, but I complied.

We found the Italian restaurant we were looking for in the community of Carlton, just a short distance from downtown Melbourne. When we walked in, the middle-aged waiter approached us wearing a distant smile. He politely seated us. The other customers then proceeded to give us the silent inspection. Many Australian restaurants don't put water on the table unless requested. When the pizza arrived we all dug in with the waiter assisting with the setup. It was a good dinner meal complete with good dinner wine. We enjoyed our meal so much that the four of us didn't realize it was nearly 20:30, only one and a half hours before the bars would be closing in Melbourne. The waiter came back to the table with the bill. Bruce insisted on picking up the tab. As Chief Steward I guess he wanted to designate himself as leader of the pack. Between the three of us Jesse, Charlie, and I left about 12 dollars for the waiter. As we walked out of the door we saw several other waiters crowding around the waiter that served us. They were smiling and speaking in Italian as they examined the money we left behind. It's a good chance they had never seen American money before. They waved at us wishing us a safe trip back to America.

In the taxi, I convinced my three shipmates to accompany me to another community I heard of, called Fitzroy. The main drag was called Gertrude Street. When we got there, my shipmates refused to get out of the taxi. Some policemen were entering pubs and some were coming out. The driver could see we were feeling uncomfortable so he volunteered to take us to a place downtown just off Elizabeth Street. We all agreed.

We were warmly received at our next stop. The driver had already told us that if we encountered any difficulty, that he would be happy to drive us down Sydney Road to Brunswick or Coburg where he knew of several Greek clubs. That's when I learned that the Greeks outnumbered all other ethnic groups in Melbourne and maybe all of Australia. Italians also number heavily, as do people from the former Yugoslavia. In spite of all these immigrants from Europe, something like six million since World War II, I think the British and Irish are still in the majority. We declined the invitation to Brunswick or Coburg, especially Coburg, the site of a notorious Australian jail. We all decided that maybe we'd sample Greek hospitality some other time. After we entered the club we took note that most of the customers were a bit younger than us. That didn't really matter. Bruce, Charlie, and I each had one beer. Jesse went for scotch as expected. I still say Australia has some of the best beer in the world outside Germany and Holland.

The dance floor was filled with people dancing in groups. Finally a slow number came up and I tried my luck. My dance partner was an attractive young lady. She welcomed me to Melbourne. When we returned to the table I noticed that two girls and a guy had invited themselves to sit with us. I must say that the taxi driver had steered us on the right course. This pub stayed open later than 10:00 PM. That meant that we didn't have to taxi across the bridge into Port Melbourne. Bruce, Charlie, and Jesse sat out all the dances but they were still enjoying themselves. It was a friendly crowd of people. Another young lady joined us at the table as I splurged on a round of drinks. As the night wore on the crowd grew merrier, but it was obvious that the relationships with the ladies at our table would only be platonic. They invited us to go out to St. Kilda to meet some friends of theirs, but we politely declined. After all, our day would be starting early tomorrow. That's one of the unpleasant things about working in the Steward Department.

The pizza dinner in Carlton put a good bottom in my stomach. I was beginning to feel a buzz from the alcohol. The four of us thanked the ladies and gentleman at the table for their hospitality and bid them goodnight. We walked the short distance to Elizabeth Street, a busy thoroughfare, and hailed a taxi to the ship. As we got in the taxi I noticed a historic looking building at the end of Elizabeth Street. As we turned right on Flinders Street I asked the taxi the name of the building to satisfy my curiosity. He told me it was the train station. We continued heading toward Spencer Street. I suspected the driver was heading in the wrong direction to get to the ship. He confessed that he had made a wrong turn and was heading in the direction of a place called Footscray.

Jesse laughed and said, "What a name! Footscray!"

I told them suburbia in Melbourne had odd sounding names just like back in the States.

"I met a guy on the docks this morning that lives in a place named Sunshine."

There was another bout of laughter.

"Buzz, you're not lying to us are you?" asked Bruce, hardly able to control his laughter.

"No," I said. "There is a Sunshine, Victoria in Australia."

They continued to laugh.

Then I asked the driver, "Am I telling the truth?"

"Yes mates, there certainly is a place here by that name."

He seemed to be getting a pleasure out of verifying it, as he made his way to the ship. He was very careful not to make any more wrong turns. Before long we were on the docks near the gangway. I could tell by the friendly smile on his middle-aged face the driver was very well satisfied with the large tip we dropped on him.

"Thank you and enjoy Australia," was his parting remark.

4

BRISBANE

The next day was routine. Many in the Deck and Engine Departments went ashore to top off on liquid refreshments. Dale and Jake were the only ones from the Steward Department to go back ashore. I suggested they try the pub we attended the night before. After dinner many of the crew watched television in the crew lounge as did some of the officers up topside. We were all looking forward to parting company with Melbourne the next morning and setting sail for Brisbane, Queensland; for better or for worse.

In Brisbane we tied up in the suburbs of Hamilton. Many of the crew got no farther than the local pub. In spite of a weekend approaching, quite a few of them stayed put. My friends and I decided to wait and venture out on the town Saturday night. That first night in town, we just went to the Hamilton Hotel pub which was within walking distance from the ship. We entered the pub just after 19:00. It was crowded with local Australians and seafarers from ships from other ports around the world. It was a friendly crowd, with only one drawback. There weren't nearly as many girls present as in the pubs in Sydney or Melbourne. But then, one would expect this kind of atmosphere in such a working class community in suburbia.

I went ashore with the same crowd as in Melbourne plus one extra: K.O. had decided to come along. He and Bruce talked briefly about adding to, or deleting, this or that from Sunday's menu. We didn't mingle with the locals. As a group, we got a few stares here and there. We each sported a round of drinks while observing the female scenery then before we realized the clock was saying 21:40. As in Melbourne, the bars would be closing at 22:00. We had one more round before taking a slow walk back to the ship and into bed. After finding a newspaper one of the dock workers had left in the lounge, I decided to stay up maybe another hour reading. It was almost like reading a paper in the States including some favorable and unfavorable articles and editorials on the war in Vietnam. After all Australia was an ally with the United States in Vietnam, but a number of

Australians did not echo the sentiments of the government. They held demonstrations and waved signs which read, "Make love not war." While reading the newspaper I took notice that the news media in Brisbane was a lot more conservative than Sydney or Melbourne.

The next day after lunch I walked to the nearby Seamen's Club to mail some cards and letters. Some to the States and one letter to Judy back in Sydney. I spent my whole three hour break at the Club getting in touch with out-of-town friends and relatives. I knew full well that after we left Brisbane it would be a few days at sea before the next port.

After serving dinner, our gang cleaned up and headed out for a night on the town. We wanted to explore some territory beyond Hamilton or Albion. I asked the taxi if he knew of a pub that was lively but not riotous and out of control and, or course, where women were not scarce.

To our delight his answer was, "Oh yes." He put his foot on the gas and headed toward Fortitude Valley better known as "the Valley." When reaching the strip he slowed down almost to a stop as he said, "This is a pub where funny men go. I don't think you want to go in there."

"Hell no!" said Jesse breaking his silence.

We all laughed including the driver.

On down the street there was another pub where the driver said, "Mostly seniors and a few middle-aged workers hang out here."

"Sorry, no liniment tonight," Charlie said.

There was laughter again. Then the driver said jokingly, "I understand. I'll keep my foot on the petrol."

As we passed through the Valley we saw a number of other pubs that didn't look too promising. We simply gave them a miss. Finally the taxi stopped in front of one pub that looked kind of promising called *Smiling Faces*. The place was nearly full of young adults and a few middle-aged couples. The taxi driver, smiling, saw us go in before taking off. Of course we felt a bit uncomfortable but before long we realized that our fears were unfounded. That pub was being true to its name. Almost all of those overwhelmingly Anglo Saxon faces were smiling, at least that night. Several men came to the table to compliment us on how well dressed we were.

One of them put a hand on my coat sleeve and said, "Enjoy your evening. Nobody will give you trouble here."

With such assurances I went to the next table where three young guys and two ladies were sitting. I asked one of the ladies for a dance but she politely declined saying she only danced with her brand new husband. She went on to explain that she would make an exception with close male friends, but never a stranger. Not to be undone, I asked the young lady at her right who gladly accepted as she giggled. The band did a slow number then an oldies-but-goodies twist from the early 60's. When we returned to the table I noticed that three more ladies had come to the table. They were friends of the people already seated. They asked me to join them. The guys were in complete agreement. I then told my three shipmates I'd make my own way back to the ship. I promised Bruce this would not be a repeat of Sydney. He laughed and said it better not be. I moved to the next table my dancing partner, Paula, introduced me to the others including Jennifer, the lovely lady who declined my request for a dance earlier. Her brand new husband's name was Ian. Later, two Maori ladies came in with their Australian boyfriends. I got Jesse's attention and touched the back of my hand.

He laughed and said, "Buzz, get the hell out of here with that jive ass sh**!"

"Yes, those girls look good," I replied.

In a little while my three shipmates were on the dance floor. They were having a whale of a time. Some girls had joined their table. The next time I looked around Charlie was touching me on the shoulder to say the three of them were leaving. They had a ride back with the girls from their table after a whirl through downtown Brisbane. It was kind of customary for people to pub crawl on a Saturday night. The girls were acting quite lively with a buzz, but seemed to be in control of themselves, at least the driver, who I was most concerned about. She told me not to worry because they would surely get my shipmates back in one piece. Then Paula said that they would see that I got back to the ship okay. My three shipmates left with their new-found lady friends and I left with two carloads for a house party across town. They treated me well and a good time was had by all. I certainly didn't expect such a night in Brisbane, but sometimes the best things in life come by total surprise.

Before leaving the pub, Jennifer and Ian invited me to their home for tea the next afternoon at 4:00 PM. I had to get used to Australians referring to dinner as "tea." Ian would pick me up at the ship around 3:00 PM. Both of his parents would be there. I talked it over with Bruce and Charlie. They gave the okay, saying they would be glad to cover dinner for me on the ship.

"Wear something nice. Don't go in those people's home dressed like a bum," Bruce said putting his foot down.

I assured him that I would dress accordingly.

◆   ◆   ◆

On Sunday all went well. Most of the officers and crew were ashore except those on duty. We worked right through breakfast and lunch. I had everything in place for Charlie for the dinner setup since he was covering for me. There was one more hurdle I had to jump across. That morning just after breakfast, I approached Jesse for a favor.

"Please," I said, "help me bake a sweet potato pie."

"What?" he asked.

"I got a dinner invitation and I want to surprise my host and hostess with something I know they don't serve over here," I continued. "I'll boil the sweet potatoes, if you could help me with the ingredients," I offered.

He paused for a few seconds and then came out with a surprise answer. I would not have to help him at all. As hungover as he was, he told me he would have my pie ready right after lunch. That was very nice of him especially since he had to cook some apple pies for the lunch menu. Juan had taken the morning off so Jesse was kind of busy with double duties. The *Marine Charger* had a full complement. The Union and the Company hadn't really begun to terminate the ship's officers and crew yet. That explained why we could take off and have a fellow crewmember stand in for us. Those days have long gone with the wind.

Later, Jesse called me to the Galley and handed me my sweet potato pie. Although it was all wrapped, I could still smell the aroma.

"Don't say I never did anything for you," he said, giving me a sly grin.

"Thank you so much! I'll sport you a jug in the next port."

"You don't have to do that, but if you insist, I travel expensive when it comes to whiskey."

We both laughed as I returned to the room to finish getting dressed. Ian would soon be pulling up on the dock to pick me up. As I went down the gangway, Jon, one of the 12–4 ABs on watch that night, wanted to know where I was going all dressed up like that.

I laughed as I told him, "It's almost dinner time, ashore that is." I added, "I'd miss the steak dinner onboard for a home-cooked meal anytime."

We laughed together some more. My joy and merrymaking would be short-lived. When I hit the docks I walked toward the gate. Two young Customs Agents came walking up to me seemingly out of nowhere. Their car was parked nearby. Of course they wanted to know what I had in the bag. My heart seemed to be skipping beats and my blood pressure must have risen a hundred points. I told them the truth about the invitation to dinner in Carina and my intention of surprising my host and hostess with the sweet potato pie. They laughed and told me it was an offense to bring food ashore in Australia. I could be fined five hundred dollars. I knew they had the ball in their court. What would happen if this incident got back to the Captain or to the Company back in New York? I decided quickly to humble myself by apologizing for being ignorant of these facts. They whispered to each other nodding affirmatively. They then came back to me saying they would let me go but told me to get in the car so that they could drive me outside the gate past the guard. They not only let me go, but they didn't even confiscate the pie. As we went out the gate the guard looked a little puzzled as to what was going on, but what he didn't know certainly didn't hurt him. Ian was just outside the gate waiting. I got out of the Custom Agents' car and headed for Ian's car.

"Thanks again for letting me off the hook," I said.

"You're a bright mate, enjoy your tea," was the driver's reply as they wheeled back through the gate.

◆　　　◆　　　◆

I told Ian that the Custom Agents were looking for contraband. Although I'm a non-smoker, I carried my allotted two packs of cigarettes allowed ashore. I didn't mention the pie episode. Neither he nor his family really had to know the ordeal I had just experienced.

We made our way back around through the Valley. Some parts of it looked like a ghost town. That could be expected as most pubs and shops locked up on Sundays. Some pubs in Brisbane would open for a few hours on Sunday mornings, but required the purchase of a meal. During our drive, I noticed many homes were built on stilts. I guessed it was for safety reasons in case of flooding. After sightseeing through the Valley and downtown Brisbane, we headed for Carina.

Seemingly in no time we were pulling up in the front yard of the Nelson residence. I felt comfortable when I saw that Ian and Jennifer's home was not built on stilts. I was pleasantly surprised by the immaculate layout of the house with brand new furniture all in place. After all, this young, 22 year old couple had been married less than three months. She was only a bank teller, but he was an assistant working with his father in imports and exports. Ian would show me around, but not before I handed Jennifer the sweet potato pie. She gasped and smiled. I explained to her that it was a Southern dish I hardly ever get enough of.

"Compliments go to our Second Cook, Jesse," I told her.

By that time she had recovered from the surprise enough to say, "Buzz, thank you so much. We really appreciate this."

"You're quite welcome," I replied.

Then the senior Nelsons, who had arrived earlier, stepped up for introductions.

"Buzz, my parents, Kylie and Eugene Nelson," Ian said. "Buzz is on a ship from America that's docked in Hamilton," he told his parents.

"My pleasure meeting you Mr. and Mrs. Nelson," I replied.

His father quickly corrected me by saying, "Kylie and Gene will do."

Ian asked if they would excuse us while we make a quick tour of the house.

"By all means," Gene said.

We made the rounds of the three bedrooms and two bathrooms. I could already see by the greenery and flowers in the front and back yards that Jennifer had a green thumb. In the kitchen I could smell dinner all but done. Also by my keen sense of smell I could tell we would be having roast beef. As we returned to the living room and got seated, Jennifer asked me, "What do you think of our humble abode?"

"Humble abode?" I asked. "If I had something this awesome back in the States I would immediately jump ship."

"Thanks," she said with a laugh.

Ian offered me a beer as he brought one out for himself and his father. I accepted as did Gene. Both his mother and Jennifer declined. Then Jennifer returned to the kitchen dutifully fulfilling her role as hostess and wife. The table was already set. Ian excused himself to help his attractive wife slice the beef and cut the sweet potato pie. While they were away from the living room the senior Nelsons and I engaged in small talk. I did not want to discuss politics with them but since they came out with the subject, I was forced to play along to a certain extent. Both of them said they hoped for peace in Vietnam soon. I echoed their sentiments there. Then the race problems in the United States and South Africa came up. They were appalled; at least they said they were by certain racial attitudes in both countries. They said they found apartheid or any form of racial segregation despicable. Gene then quickly admitted Australia had problems of race, but nothing of the magnitude of America and South Africa. I had held my tongue as long as I could. Then I figured it was time to come out with my two cents worth. I told them that I hope they would not be offended by what I was about to say. Kylie then said no, insisting that I speak up. I mainly directed my remarks toward Gene, telling him I agreed that Australia's race problems were not in the magnitude of those in America or South Africa. I added that a fly in the ointment was their White Australia Policy. Gene said that he opposed that policy, but he believed the Australian government imposed it to avoid some of the problems of race some other countries encountered.

"Nothing against you, Buzz," Kylie added.

She then said that some of the Europeans that came over after World War II brought problems along with them. I didn't question her on that point.

Gene said, "Buzz, with your intelligence you can hold your own in any part of the world. I wish you would come back here to stay awhile."

"We would be happy to have you," Kylie added.

"Thanks, but America is my home," I said. "That's where I was born and I have no intention of living any place else; not even Africa where my roots are. I may visit other parts of the world as part of my job, but America will always be home to me through the best and worst of times."

"Let us know if you change your mind. We'll do what we can to help you."

Through all of our discussions I never heard the "N" word used, nor did I ever hear the word "Wog," a derogatory word used for some Europeans. When the subject of Dr. Martin Luther King Jr. came up, they wanted my opinion. I told them I admired his accomplishments especially that as a Nobel Laureate. Adding that I hoped he lives to be no longer needed in the field of civil rights and can one day return to the pulpit. Gene said he doubted that would be any time soon.

Just then Ian and Jennifer called us to the table. Everything in their small dining room off the kitchen was right in place. It was as immaculate as the rest of the house. Ian insisted I be seated at the head of the table. Jennifer said grace and the meal was on. What a tea it was! The seating arrangement had both couples sitting side by side and across from each other. I could tell the hot dinner rolls came from scratch. The green peas and spring onions were a good substitute for salad. Everything was just awesome, even the dark gravy for the roast beef and boiled potatoes. We went through dinner with general conversation about family. I learned that Gene and Kylie had four other children: two boys and two girls. Ian was the youngest. As they rattled off the names of their other children I made a good guess that they were a family of English background. Jennifer on the other hand came from a smaller family, just parents and two brothers. She is the oldest of the children. Her parents lived nearby, working in the Brisbane schools. I told them how I envied them for having such settled family lives. They laughed as Gene told me my life may change one day, if I would ever tire of my globetrotting habits.

"Food for thought," I said as I laughed and went on devouring the hearty meal.

Soon my plate was about empty. Jennifer noticed and asked what else she could get for me. I told her to please fix me another order of roast beef and peas. I was not embarrassed since Ian also was finishing, and ordered seconds on everything. Soon everybody was finished with the main course. Jennifer then announced that she was serving the sweet potato pie for dessert. "Oohs" and "Ahhs" went around the table. I already felt I was about to burst around the seams, but I had to force a piece down. Jennifer begged forgiveness until Kylie persuaded her to share a slice with her. Gene and Ian each had a slice. They all told me how delicious it was. It was the first time any of them had eaten sweet potato pie. Right away Jennifer wanted the recipe. I told her I didn't know all the ingredients, but would get them from Jesse and mail it to her from the next port. She thanked me and they all told me to thank Jesse for them.

As we returned to the living room, I thanked them all for giving me such a wonderful evening. Ian took several beers from the refrigerator and handed me one. The senior Nelsons declined, as did Jennifer. From a pitcher in the refrigerator, Jennifer poured three glasses of punch for her in-laws and herself. We made after dinner small talk for nearly an hour. Gene and Kylie invited me to come back for an extended holiday there. At first I was surprised, then I remembered that Australians use the word "holiday" instead of "vacation." I assured them that I would, one of these days. Although I knew it would be no time soon. Gene and Kylie then apologized for having to leave saying they had promised earlier to call on several friends on their way home. They again asked me to come back for a visit. Before walking out the front door Gene gave me a firm handshake and Kylie and I warmly embraced.

After his parents left, Ian assured me that he would drive me back to the ship and told me to be in no hurry to leave. I tarried another hour until it was nearly 8:30 PM. I came up with an idea.

I told Ian, "You both see me back and I'll take you on a whirlwind tour of the ship."

They asked whether I was sure this could happen.

"Let's try," I said and in no time we were on our way to Hamilton Dock.

The tour of the ship was exciting for them. It was only a short walk from the gate to the gangway. Since sea watch would not be set until midnight, Lester was still on duty.

"Hello Buzz," said Lester as we came aboard. He eyed Jennifer from head to toe.

I asked him if I could show my friends around. I assured him their visit would be short.

"Sure, be my guest, just be careful getting around," he said as he gave us a friendly smile.

The Captain's rule was that I couldn't show them the Bridge of the ship so we went straight to the Crew Mess. It was empty. Many of the crew and officers were either in bed already or still ashore. I showed them a menu after we were seated. They were very surprised at the many entrees and vegetables we had to choose from. Just then Eddy, one of the Engine Department's wipers, showed up in the Mess Hall with the platter of night lunch from the refrigerator. He fixed himself a ham and cheese sandwich and asked me to watch it, saying he would be right back. When he got back he had three cold Budweisers from the cooler in his room. He offered each of us a beer. As expected, Jennifer politely declined. Ian confessed he had never had an American beer and was anxious to try one. He assured me he was in good driving condition. Determined that Jennifer would not be left out, I went to the refrigerator and pulled out a pitcher of iced tea and some lemon slices. I poured her a glass from the plastic pitcher. She thanked me as she refused sugar. Ian sipped his Budweiser.

"Not bad," he said, but I could tell he was just being polite.

I finished my beer knowing that there would be no more alcohol for me that night. After the introductions, Eddy told Jennifer and Ian about his father and the good times he enjoyed while stationed in Sydney as a young soldier during World War II. They were impressed. Eddy also told them how his father spoke of Australians as having the same strong family values as Americans he left back in North Carolina.

"Thank you," said Jennifer while sipping her iced tea.

Ian then told how his grandparents spoke of American servicemen who had come to the aid of Australians during World War II. Eddy had been to Australia a few times before and said each visit made him want to come back again and again. He was in his late twenties and was looking forward to bringing his wife back there on vacation. Ian and Jennifer thought such an idea would be wonderful.

We chatted in the Crew Recreation Room for about an hour until Jennifer reminded Ian that it was just past 10:00 PM and tomorrow was Monday. It would be a busy working day at the bank for her and at the office for Ian.

"A busy day for us also since we're setting sail at 10:00 AM," I said while pointing at Eddy, then at myself.

Eddy told Ian and Jennifer what a pleasure it was to meet them. I thanked Eddy for the beer and he headed for his room. I then took my guests on a quick tour of the Officer's Mess and showed them back to the gangway. As the three of us went out on deck, Jennifer's long blonde hair took on a special glow in the bright lights. She and Ian certainly made a nice looking couple. They thanked me saying how they enjoyed their visit to the ship.

"I enjoyed the visit and dinner at your home even better," I replied.

Lester was still on watch at the gangway. He and about five more officers and crew stood by as I saw my guests down the gangway and across to the gate.

"I wish we were going to New Zealand," Ian said. "Never been there."

"Neither have I," was my answer, but I bet them it would not be as exciting as Australia.

At the gate Ian and I shook hands and Jennifer and I embraced promising each other we would keep in touch.

As they drove off, back toward Carina, I noticed a taxi pulling up at the gate. There was a Black couple in the back seat. Not able to control my curiosity, I went a little closer toward the taxi. The couple was the Bos'n, Bob Harris, and his young Fijian girlfriend, Yasmin. He had been with her off and on all weekend between duties on the ship. They held hands and chatted a few minutes before she got back in the taxi. I made an about face and went back aboard before either of them recognized me.

After going up the gangway, I noticed the same guys manning the rail. They were not missing a trick. They were all White, including Lester. Not that it mattered, but some of them could not understand how the Blacks on the ship could form a relationship based on true friendship with respectable Australians. Eddy was one White man that didn't have those hang-ups; he had a mind of his own. As I walked back up the ladder, I paused briefly to look at the sailing board which read: "Ship sails 10:00 Monday December 5; Auckland, New Zealand." Most of the crew had already returned from shore, especially those in the Deck Department. The few crew members still ashore soon started straggling in. Seemingly nobody wanted to be left behind in Brisbane.

Over breakfast on Monday morning, officers and crew alike swapped sea stories but none like those told after Sydney. What a difference! After tidying up the Saloon Mess, I went to sit down awhile in the crew lounge. Jesse was there finishing a short break before returning to the Galley. I told him what a big hit the pie was with the Nelsons.

"Anytime," he said.

I went out on deck and said a "so long" to Australia. I started preparing myself for the more than one thousand nautical mile trip to New Zealand. After lunch I decided to take a nap during my three hour break. As I reclined in bed, I thought of my whirlwind trip through Australia. Mainly what I learned and what I didn't have time to learn.

I went there with mixed emotions. All my life I heard about Australia being a White man's country in the interests of Whites only. My knowledge of the White Australia Policy made me believe that I would encounter nothing but contempt if I went there, no matter how long or how short my stay. On the other hand I had talked with American servicemen of color, mostly sailors who went there on ships with the seventh fleet, who said they had had a ball. Now I could understand that. After all, plenty of wine, women, and song were available, and like me, these sailors were not there to stay.

I would love to have stayed longer to mingle with more people of different backgrounds, but my job did not permit it.

I met Whites, both Australian born and foreign born; I visited their homes and observed their very impressive family values. I also met Whites from the streets that seemed to have little or no sense of family. I met Moors, Fijians, and a few other Polynesians, but to my regret, I didn't get to meet and mingle with any Aborigines. I saw several tribesmen in Brisbane but, it would have been nice to meet them and hear them out. The Aborigines make up only one percent of the population, so they are too few in numbers to press for their civil rights causes. I visited the state capitals, Sydney, New South Wales; Melbourne, Victoria; and Brisbane, Queensland. They are the three largest cities in Australia. It's said that 90 percent of the population lives in the cities along the coast. Since I was born on a farm during the Great Depression era, I think I would have enjoyed visiting the Outback, farms, and inland deserts where the other 10 percent live. Tasmania would also have been fun, mingling with the sheep farmers and going on a pub crawl in Hobart. All that would have to wait until a later visit to the Land Down Under.

My opinion of Australia is yes, racism exists there but, "You can't always touch it," as my lady friend, Judy, said.

The Canberra government can enforce all the racial policies they want, but the warm receptions I received during my sojourn made me happy to see that many White Australians are adult enough to have minds of their own.

5

NEW ZEALAND

We encountered only smooth seas en route to Auckland. The ship's store, known as the Slop Chest, was opened our second day at sea to allow the crew to stock up on sodas, cigarettes, and other goodies. Almost everyone put in overtime while we were at sea, especially the day before entering port.

When we arrived in Auckland, New Zealand's largest city, I was happy to see that we went to Ferguson Dock. That meant we were within walking distance to downtown. It was early afternoon when we finished docking. It would be after dinner before members of the Steward Department, except the Chief Steward and Larry the BR, would be off duty and able to go out on the town. The same gang decided to go out together that night. We would leave at about 19:00. Many in the Deck and Engine Departments were already ashore.

Bruce and Jesse insisted we take a taxi even after I told them it was only a short distance to city center. We had barely gotten seated in the taxi and were speeding down the waterfront, when the Maori driver pulled up in front of a club and assured us this was where much of the action was. This club was located near Queen Street, one of the main drags downtown. As we stepped out of the taxi one could not help noticing the variety of people walking by on the street. Some of them were respectable looking White and Polynesian New Zealanders while others were an assortment of streetwalkers, hustlers, and female impersonators.

We were all laughing as we entered the club. All of us, except Charlie, were casually dressed. He was dressed as sharp as usual, in one of his gray summer suits. This club, called *Lenny's*, catered to a crowd of straight laced, fun loving people. I was quite happy to see that the bouncers, both Maori, were keeping a close vigil and would tolerate no nonsense. The crowd was mixed. Whites, Maori, Tongans, and other Polynesians were all represented here. They appeared friendly but the four of us stood out like a sore thumb. It was clear to all that we were visitors rather than locals. Occasionally, some of the guests would give a friendly wave to our table. The girls were nice looking, but there were a few who were outwardly attractive with unbecoming personalities. Some of the women were trying to keep up with the men as far as drinking goes. A good time was still being had by all. When looking at those Maori girls, my thoughts went back to Judy who I left behind in Sydney. One of them looked so much like her they could have passed for sisters.

Several girls were standing next to the wall. I asked Jesse if he thought they wanted to sit down. Without answering me, he went over and asked them. They accepted our invitation and were soon followed by three more girls. Seemingly, I had started the ball rolling. To my satisfaction, they were respectable girls. It didn't take us long to get acquainted. The music was good and many in the pub were in a dancing mood. Most were local residents, but I met one couple from Wellington, New Zealand's capital city. They wanted to know whether we were enjoying our stay in Auckland. I told them we were, but regretfully we would be there only two days.

At the table the party was on. Bruce, as usual, was the lowest keyed. Charlie, in spite of being the oldest in the party, was the most active. Jesse was the loudest, and in spite of being the youngest I found myself trying to keep up. The older men didn't sit out too many dance numbers. The combo was wailing on and time was passing quickly. I have a talent for meeting people and learning as much as I can about a place in a short period of time. I struck up a meaningful conversation with Hailey, one of the girls at the table. We went on the dance floor for several fast numbers. I could barely keep up with her, but it was nice trying. The mood was festive all through the evening. I was surprised to learn how easy it was to meet girls. They were girls who were ready for a party.

The boss, a burly Englishman, came to our table and referred to us as Yanks. He motioned to the waiter, telling him to bring us a round of drinks. He told us to have a good evening and to enjoy our stay in Auckland. We all thanked him as we raised a toast. After mingling briefly with some other customers he continued on his way to his office.

The music was sounding better all the time. It was a mix of local and American music I remembered well from years gone by. Earlier in the evening we decided to pub crawl, going to as many clubs as we had time to patronize, but after this warm reception at *Lenny's* we changed our minds. It was almost 11:00 PM when we decided to hold on to what we had and not go chasing birds in other bushes.

My conversation with Hailey turned serious as she spoke of being estranged from her boyfriend, not a surprising statement from a young lady of 25. She had to be at work at a restaurant across town by 7:00 AM the next morning so I offered to see her home. She accepted. Before leaving *Lenny's*, we invited the girls at the table to visit the ship our last night in port. Some of them declined, but three of them, including Hailey, said they would think about it. Good enough. Within five minutes Hailey and I were saying goodnight to the others at the table. Jesse was walking out right behind us with his new-found lady friend. Both Bruce and Charlie returned to the ship empty handed.

On our way to Hailey's apartment, the taxi drove slowly through downtown traffic. He cut off on a side street and seemingly in no time we were at Hailey's door. Unlike Judy, she was living alone. Her one bedroom apartment was neat and as clean as a whistle. I spotted some men's clothing in one of her closets. She could read the curious look on my face and started to explain. She told me not to worry about him coming in. She had given him walking papers because he wouldn't work, developed a drinking problem, and had become a financial burden on her. Now that she was caught up with her rent and slowly catching up with other bills, she could see light at the end of the tunnel. When she went in the powder room I did some snooping. I saw a receipt on her coffee table. She had been allowed to pay half of her rent that month. Imagine my shock when I discovered the rent on her apartment was only 40 dollars a month. Here was a hard working young woman trying to pay her own way. Her parents were keeping her four year old son who she was also supporting off a minimum wage job. Those type of women I would walk the whole mile with rather than walk two steps with some street hustler. Oh, I would meet plenty of girls walking the streets, but I would only manage to tolerate those that didn't rock the boat.

When Hailey came out of the powder room, I told her we had to have a talk. I told her if she put me up for the night I would make it worth her while. She smiled and said she liked the pleasure of my company and I owed her nothing. Then she thanked me for the drinks I bought for her all evening. I assured her the pleasure was all mine. She offered me a drink, but I declined. We both had had enough. She gave me a good party, such a good party I forgot to remind her of my obligation for an early rise the next morning. As it turned out, I didn't have to. Just after 5:30 AM she was nudging me. It was a real task for me to get out of that soft, comfortable bed, but I didn't want a repeat of my troubles in Sydney. I would be on time to cover my duties come what may. We both cleaned up and she offered to fix me a breakfast snack.

"No thanks," I said, "I can eat on the ship."

The water was boiling and she poured herself a cup of tea. Everything had to run like clockwork since we both had places to go. I insisted we sit at the kitchen table for a few minutes. I didn't let her know that I had looked at her receipts, I just asked her how far behind she was in her rent. She said she would pay it off on payday, which was in three days.

"Let's strike a deal," I suggested.

"You use your payday to pay off your back rent, then when it's due again in little more than two weeks, that's where I come in."

I took 40 dollars from my pocket and put it on the table. She told me how nice I had been and wanted to know why I was doing that since we had just met. I reminded her how nice we had been to each other and assured her that I could afford it. She grudgingly accepted the money as she thanked me, she bussed me on both cheeks. I commented that her rent would not be due again for six weeks now. She laughed as she counted and recounted the bills. She had not seen very much American currency. She made a comment that all Yank money was the same color. She kept thanking me over and over. By that time the taxi she had called was there. She would see me to the taxi then walk down the street to catch a bus to work. I would hear no such thing. I told her we would both take the same taxi. The driver could take me back to the ship and then take her to work at my expense.

"Oh, no," she said.

"Oh, yes," I said as I got out of the taxi at Ferguson Dock. I gave her a kiss and we made arrangements to meet at *Lenny's* at 7:00 PM when I would bring her aboard ship for a brief visit.

The taxi driver was very pleased with my fare and tip.

◆   ◆   ◆

I went aboard ship and ran into Dale and Jake who were also just returning from shore. As young studs, they were wild with excitement and could not stop talking about their overnight experiences. As I served breakfast crew and officers alike were abuzz with sea stories. I could hardly keep my cool. Even the First Engineer Steve Martinjak, who was almost into his seventies, started bragging about his new girlfriend. He swore he might return to Auckland and get married. 72 year old Sully, the Chief Mate, started smiling and shaking his head as he finished breakfast and walked out of the Mess Hall. My co-worker, Charlie, had heard it all. Outside the Mess Hall, the three of us conversed in low tones.

"No fool like an old fool," Sully said.

"He better get his old ass back to that woman he's been with over 50 years," Charlie said.

"He'll come back down to earth from his new-found high and go on back into retirement," I said.

Many of the officers and crew of the *Marine Charger* had been retired 20 years or more, but came out to move cargo during the Vietnam War. Most of them were not bad off financially. They came back for sentimental reasons. Many had survived dangerous crossings and difficult experiences during World War II and the Korean Conflict. They came back to relive the good old days they experienced in years gone by. But, in most cases, those good old days were just not there anymore. Life goes on.

◆   ◆   ◆

During my three hour break after lunch, I went downtown to take care of some chores. First I went to mail some letters. I sent one, along with some money, off to my sister in South Carolina and another letter to Judy back in Sydney. Then I sent the recipe for Jesse's sweet potato pie back to Jennifer in Brisbane. After leaving the Post Office I shopped around for a few souvenirs.

As I moved around Auckland I couldn't help noticing the ethnic make up of the people. I learned that less than 80 percent of New Zealanders are of European descent; mostly British and Irish. The native Maori people make up about ten percent. The Maori have their own official language, but all of the native New Zealanders I met spoke English. The remaining percentage of the population is comprised of Tongans and other non-Whites. There has been a lot of race mixing in New Zealand over the centuries. The Whites are very much in the majority there, but the Maori citizens enjoy so many more privileges than the Aboriginal people back in Australia. Race relations are not perfect but the Maori on both the North and South Islands of New Zealand are well represented in a wide range of jobs, from taxi drivers and civil servants to law enforcement officers, business men, and educators. The Maori were also prominent in the arts, sports, and entertainment fields especially enjoying Rugby and Cricket, the national pastimes.

Just before returning to ship I got another surprise. I saw a young police officer waiting outside of a store for his partner. Just before I approached, his partner came out. They gave me a friendly greeting, but I was unable to hide the shocked look on my face. I returned their greeting then told them of my surprise. They were both armed with batons, or night sticks, but neither of them was wearing a gun. In a city this large that was something to write about. We chatted for several minutes and parted on a friendly note. I headed along the docks and back to the ship.

As I looked back to take note of them in their blue uniforms, complete with summer shorts, I asked myself, "When could policemen in the United States stroll down the streets unarmed?"

My answer was, "No time soon."

◆　　　◆　　　◆

Serving dinner was easy. Most of my shipmates were off duty and had gone ashore. When I went back ashore after dinner I stopped in several pubs. I saw some fellow crew members on the streets and in pubs downtown. Most of them were in the Deck and Engine Departments. The younger ones, had girls on their arms. I only gave them a nodding glance. I had no intention of interrupting social progress. The good times were there for the asking. Not fast paced like Sydney but more laid back where you could take your time and there would still be a party when you made up your mind.

It was time to meet Hailey at *Lenny's*. We had a round of drinks and chatted briefly with Sully and his girl. A taxi was called and almost like "1–2–3," Hailey and I were walking up the gangway. Lester was on duty and I knew that the sailing board would be posted soon.

"Have a good evening, but be careful," Lester said as he waved us on.

Some captains allowed crew members to bring women onboard and others did not. Captain Schraeder was broad-minded. He had the Bos'n pass the word on down to the crew that it was alright to bring girls aboard, but to stay with them at all times. Visitors were welcome in the crew lounge or in our rooms, but were not allowed to run around the ship unescorted. After all, accidents could happen. We all complied.

By just after 20:00 there were 15 to 20 girls aboard ship. They were all attractive and well mannered. Most of them were escorted aboard by members of the crew while a few others came along with friends from the pubs. We turned the crew lounge into a makeshift bar bringing extra chairs from the rooms.

Unlike Merchant vessels from England, Australia, and New Zealand, American Merchant ships don't have bars aboard. Alcohol is not allowed aboard, but on most occasions if the Seaman does his job and doesn't make trouble the officials up topside will lay off.

Some of the crew and a few officers joined in. One contributed a jug of whiskey he picked up while he was ashore earlier. I brought a jug of rum and split a case of Cokes with Charlie. I hurried to the Galley and returned with two bowls of sliced lemons. Martinjak was there with his young girlfriend. It was considered no big thing that there was nearly a 50 year age difference. He and the young Third Engineer, Jason, were the only officers at the party. Some others from topside came down but, after gawking a few seconds, passed on through. The ice machine was kicking out ice big time and we had four plastic buckets filled with cold American, Australian, and New Zealand beers. That was more than enough since most of the guests were drinking whiskey. A few of the girls were mixing Cubre Libros or gin n' tonics. Bruce came in with a tray of onion dip and an assortment of other hors d'oeuvres he had fixed earlier. K.O. brought in his girlfriend. Not surprisingly, she was an Irish New Zealander. He was of Irish descent also, but a half world away culturally. She was beautiful and they made a handsome couple. All the while we were setting up the party the girls looked on impressed. We even hooked up some music thanks to Brad, the Electrician. The party was on and the crew lounge was filled. Just when the party was getting started, in walked Bob the Bos'n. He talked and mingled among the crowd thanking the girls for gracing us seafarers with their presence.

"Let me know if you encounter any trouble," he told them.

The girls thanked him and assured Bob they were enjoying themselves. By that time Jesse was about on cloud nine and had begun to get loud.

Bob went straight over to Jesse and said, "Don't rock the boat. The Captain and Chief Officer Sullivan could come down and break up the party if you get out of hand," he reminded him. "Anybody who messes up," he warned, looking around the room, "will have my Black ass to whip."

"Okay," Jesse said.

With that said, Bob and his young lady friend made their exit. Hailey only had one drink then switched to 7-Up with a twist of lemon. We chatted about different things. One of them was how her friends and coworkers tried to talk her out of coming to the ship. She had no regrets.

"Good to know you have a mind of your own," I said.

Then the subject of race relations came up. Hailey had heard about the racial problems in the United States and tried to keep up with the news on the subject.

"You all seem to get along alright," she said pointing out the men at the party.

"With all of these lovely girls around tonight you're darn right we're getting along," I joked.

She found the statement amusing and asked, "What is the racial make up of the ship's crew?"

I thought for a minute and told her, "There are only seven of us Blacks onboard. Two of us hold positions of authority: the Chief Steward and the Bos'n. They're in charge of a group of men and, having sailed for a number of years, are very gifted in their lines of work."

"What's your job?"

I told her I was working at an entry rating. My job was to serve three meals a day in the Saloon Mess as well as keep it clean and tidy. I then pointed to Charlie and told her he was my working partner. All officers, about 14 in total, were White and overwhelmingly Anglo Saxon. All of them were from the East Coast where the ship crewed up. Hailey then wanted to know how I got along with them. I told her I got along by doing my job and being courteous and polite. I pointed out Dale and Jake and told Hailey they worked in the same capacity as I did, but they took care of the crew. I also told her they were getting off after one more voyage to return to school at the University of Oregon. She was amazed when I told her that there were a few Blacks who refused to work on ships traveling to Australia because of its racial policies, but yet they would risk their lives to ship out to Vietnam for the bonus pay.

"To each his own," I said.

We continued chatting for little more than an hour. Just before 23:00 the crowd began to thin out. My shipmates had either retreated to their rooms with their lady friends or gone back downtown. To my surprise, there was not much of a mess from the party. The Second Mate, Sheehan, drifted through on his watch. We had the crew lounge all cleaned up in ten minutes and caught a taxi at the foot of the gangway. Martinjak put his lady friend in a taxi with some of her friends and handed the driver a handsome fare and tip. He then went back up topside to bed. He was in no condition to go back ashore. Jesse returned ashore with his lady even though he was feeling no pain. Neither Bruce nor Charlie went back ashore. The younger crew members headed for *Lenny's* and other pubs downtown. Midnight was fast approaching and Hailey and I agreed to skip the pub crawl and head straight to her place. It would be a repeat performance of the night before, except we talked for a short while. I was curious about her background. She told me she had possibly a thousand years ancestral background in New Zealand. I reminded her that wouldn't be possible since the Whites didn't start coming into New Zealand until the 1800's. Then she lowered the boom. She looked like a White woman with her fair complexion and brown hair, but looks can be deceiving. Her mother was Maori and the Maoris had been in New Zealand for a thousand years. Her father was Scots-Irish, a newcomer. I told her it didn't matter, but I must say that I had had enough fact finding for one night.

We had scones and tea together bright and early the next morning. They were very tasty. I took out about 26 dollars and put it on her table. The Queen's image showed clearly on both the bills and the coins. It was left over currency I had exchanged several days earlier and wouldn't need since we were on our way out of the country. New Zealand seems to follow the English system even more than other commonwealth countries, including Australia. I kept a few dollars for the taxi back to the ship. Then I added an American ten dollar bill.

"Are you sure?" Hailey asked when she saw the money.

I assured her I was, and reminded her of how nice she had been to me during my stay in Auckland. If anybody wanted to accuse me of being a sugar daddy, so be it. She picked up the American currency and examined it closely just as she had done the morning before. She thanked me repeatedly, and said I had almost made her debt free. She owed a few bills here and there, but all in small denominations. Again, I told her the pleasure was all mine.

As I got out of the taxi on the dock, Hailey told me we might go to a theater to see a show or concert on my next visit. As I kissed her goodbye she looked misty eyed. I told her we also would have a meal in one of Auckland's exclusive restaurants. I then told the taxi to see her to her job and waved another goodbye. As I walked up the gangway, I read the sailing board: "Papeete, Tahiti." I realized Hailey meant more to me than just another girl in another port.

The ship would sail at 08:00 so I handed a letter to one of the dockworkers who promised to mail it for me. It was going to Betty back in San Francisco. I offered him a tip, but the gentleman said he would be happy to mail my letter and refused compensation. In two hours we were on our way out of the harbor.

◆   ◆   ◆

It was smooth sailing to the beautiful, French Polynesian port of Tahiti. We arrived there early on Sunday afternoon. The French presence was very evident. There were American and French tourists and a horde of French sailors. Why worry? There would be room enough for all and we would only be there for an overnight stay. We went to some clubs in Papeete, but it was not Auckland by a long shot. The atmosphere was not the same. I missed the girls of Auckland like Hailey and my shipmates' girls like Jodie and Alice. Jesse came along to check out the clubs and so did Bob. Two of my drinking buddies, Bruce and Charlie stayed aboard. It was déjà vu for them. We all made do with what we had: rubbing shoulders with tourists, enjoying the tropical drinks, and dancing with the local girls. They were fairly friendly but in a way, distant. So many of these tourists were spending big money for their vacations, they hardly had the time for some passing seafarers. Then again, many of them were already coupled off. I stumbled up to an attractive Polynesian girl, Denise. She spoke fluent French, to no surprise. I had taken French in high school and college and liked having the chance to practice a little. She was in a friendly mood and accepted my request for a dance. My shipmates had ventured off to other bars or back to the ship. I asked Denise to call me Buzz. She was a respectable young lady working at one of the resort hotels and making her own way. We conversed back and forth in faltering English and French. She wanted to know how many years of French I had taken.

"Quatre ans, mais beaucoup des ans passé," I answered. Translated, I said, "Four years, but many years ago."

We had a nice conversation, but later I accepted the fact that she was not going to the ship with me. Nor was she going to take me home. By then it was near midnight. I offered her another drink, but she declined saying she would be having an early day at work. I understood. She walked with me to the taxi stand which was about a block away. We chatted a few minutes before a taxi pulled up. She was going to the hotel where she worked and would hitch a ride home with friends. We embraced only as new-found friends would do.

"Bon voyage," she said, as I got in the taxi.

"Merci et autre fois," I said, as the driver pulled away toward the ship.

6

HOLIDAYS

We set sail the next morning, heading nonstop to the Canal Zone. The crew was a bit puzzled. We had been scheduled to go to San Francisco, but orders changed. Instead of San Francisco, we would go to Balboa on the Pacific side, docking briefly at Rodman Naval Station. The crew was excited. The first two days at sea were full of all kinds of gossip over breakfast, lunch, and dinner. It was announced that the ship was now under government contract commonly known as M.S.C., or Military Sealift Command. We would be hauling Military cargo to the bases in the Far East; which bases, we wouldn't know just yet. Maybe we would find out more in Panama. We all knew one thing for sure. After the cargo was loaded the *S.S. Marine Charger* would be heading to ports in Japan and Vietnam. We would be in for a long haul especially with the monsoon season not yet over. I wondered why we didn't load up on the West Coast, but the government had issued its orders and that was that. No arguments.

After arriving in Panama, most of the crewmen were ready to party, especially after such a short stay in Tahiti. Two days of fun it was. Just about anything and everything was available, for a price. The girls in the bars were attractive for the most part, and, if I might add, quite friendly.

"You buy me drink?" started the conversation followed by a get together for a small fee.

Don't get me wrong, not all Panamanians are like this. Many of them, whether well-off or poor, have family values and are living lives of decency and self-respect. But we didn't make contact with any of them. In the places we patronized, bar hustlers and street wise people were available in abundance. One thing's for sure, hardly anybody was lonely. The attitude was "let the good times roll" and roll they did! I had decided to go out on the town the first night in port and chill on the second night. I did just that, ending up partying with the girls but only in a platonic sort of way. I enjoyed my evening but not the same way that I enjoyed Auckland and Sydney. It was a different atmosphere altogether.

The next morning in the Mess Hall most of my crewmates came forth with an assortment of sea stories. Some of them would make you laugh while others would make you shake your head in disbelief. Neither our boss Bruce, nor Charlie, went ashore. Charlie pleaded fatigue while Bruce was getting too close to home to take any chances. Jesse went out and partied the night away. He had been with a nice looking girl, but he was all hung-over at breakfast. He managed to drag himself through the morning and noon meals, then went to bed for several hours, as did Ken, the Galley Man. Juan, the Third Cook, was as cool as ever. You could hardly tell he had been ashore the night before. 20 years of Navy discipline had rubbed off on him.

I had decided to pass on going ashore the next night, but ended up going along with several other crewmates to the Enlisted Club on base. It was less of a rat race than the bar in town. Everybody was polite and the drinks were cheap, all in all a good evening. It was good visiting Panama again. Returning to the ship just before midnight I could see the sailing board hadn't changed. It still read: "Bayonne, New Jersey." I didn't mind the coastwise trip, but most everybody in the crew realized we would be at sea a few extra days which meant that Christmas would be spent at sea just before we reached Bayonne.

◆   ◆   ◆

We transited the canal which I think is always a sight to behold, stopped briefly in Cristobol, then got through the locks without incident. Those mechanical mules are something awful, never missing a trick. The hours it took getting from the Pacific side to the Atlantic side was amazing, of course I couldn't observe it all due to duty obligations, but I observed what I could. After Cristobol on the Atlantic side, it was full steam ahead. Captain Schraeder could have his meals in the Saloon Mess instead of having Larry the BR serve him on the Bridge. Things were going about routine onboard, the fire and boat drill had gone down right after Cristobol. We were now sailing up the East Coast and Christmas was only two days away. Here we were returning to the States in the middle of winter. The crew was in a festive mood. Many of them had stocked up on goodies and other refreshment at Panama.

Bruce Williams and Kevin "K.O." O'Keefe got together to plan the Christmas feast. These two men got along like two peas in a pod in spite of the fact that Bruce was almost 30 years older than K.O. The main reason, as I saw it, for their close relationship was the fact that K.O. was one of the best Chief Cooks in the Merchant fleet and was always there when the Steward needed him. After doing an Army hitch as a cook in 1963, K.O. decided to attend a culinary arts school in Boston. When he graduated the following year, he left his hometown of Quincy, Massachusetts for New York where he managed to obtain his Seaman documents and joined the Merchant Marines; much to the objection of his new wife. Within two years K.O. was Chief Cook making his rounds from passenger ships to freighters. Bruce allowed K.O. to mostly run things his own way in the Galley. Between the two of them and the back-up assistance of Jesse, Juan, and Ken, that Christmas meal was going to be one of the best ever served aboard the *Marine Charger.*

◆   ◆   ◆

Christmas Day fell on a Sunday that year. Engine wipers and other day workers were off all weekend, and many got Monday off too. The watch standers and anyone in the Deck, Engine, or Steward Departments still did their regular duties. It was mostly routine duty but we were getting overtime pay for the holiday weekend, which I grabbed up at every opportunity. Saturday night was busy for Bruce and K.O. The rest of us in the department volunteered our services in fixing the hors d'oeuvres and placing them neatly back in the chill box for the next day.

We knocked off around 22:00 retreating to K.O.'s room for a Christmas Eve toast. He was a generous host offering up his Irish whiskey, but only Dale and Jake accepted. Then he broke out a jug of bourbon.

"Now you're talking," I said, as I grabbed a 7-Up out of the case for a chaser.

Bruce, Charlie, Lenny, and Juan went on to bed. Ken had a beer and a shot of bourbon before retiring for the night. Jesse, Dale, Jake, and I stayed up until just after midnight welcoming in another Christmas. My first voyage was almost over. The payoff would be two days later in Bayonne, New Jersey. We all started to leave knowing what a busy task we all had before us the next day, but K.O. insisted we have another round. He proposed a toast to the next voyage which we all guessed would be back to the West Coast and across the Pacific Ocean to the Far East and Southeast Asia. We were all happy to know that nobody in the Steward Department would be joining the "Suitcase Brigade." Suitcase Brigades occurred at the end of a voyage when seafarers were fired or left the ship under mutual consent. They would leave with luggage in tow as they walked down the gangway. Some of them looking shame faced for their misbehavior such as drunkenness, fighting, and other offenses. They were usually among the first in line for payoff.

Jesse and K.O. were among the happiest guys in the room, with good reasons. Their wives would be meeting them in Bayonne. Since Jesse lived on Long Island, he and his wife would go on home for a day and night. We would only be in Bayonne for two days so K.O. and his wife spent their time in a New York motel. It was nice of Bruce and Jesse to invite us West Coasters for a short visit to their respective homes, but we all declined since they had such little time with their families while we were in port.

◆   ◆   ◆

The Christmas dinner was, as usual, served at lunchtime. The hors d'oeuvres, from stuffed celery to deviled eggs, were laid out on spare tables in each Mess Hall. That meal was fit for anybody's royalty. Young Tom turkey, dressing, and giblet gravy topped the entrees with roast beef and au jus a close second. Not to forget the Virginia baked ham glazed with pineapple sauce. Mashed potatoes and gravy, asparagus, and green peas filled in the vegetable list. The cream of tomato soup was really out of sight. Apple pie a la mode and pumpkin pie were knock-outs for desserts. Crew and officers alike ate like there would be no tomorrow. Some old fogies on the ship, that usually bitched and griped at other meals, sat at the table and pigged out eating seconds and thirds of dessert.

After the meal was over, Captain Schraeder stopped by the Galley on the way to his quarters. He personally thanked Bruce for a job well done, getting the meal out and doing such a super job as head of the Steward Department. Then he turned to K.O. and offered his personal thanks telling him the Christmas dinner was one of the best shipboard spreads he had experienced in all his years at sea. The Captain also thanked the other two cooks, Jesse and Juan, as well as the Galley Man Ken.

"Thank you, Captain," they courteously replied, accepting his compliment.

The Captain even thanked us four Messmen in the Crew and Saloon Mess Halls for serving a great meal and complimented how nice the Christmas trees were decorated. The Captain then took a stroll on through the Crew Mess Hall wishing them all a Merry Christmas, as he continued to his quarters. These compliments to the Steward Department would be repeated all day by officers and crew alike: Chief Mate Sully, Chief Engineer Grassi, First Engineer Martinjak, Second Mate Sheehan, Radio Officer Grayson, Bos'n Bob, and Wiper Eddy to name a few. The same meal would be served again at 17:00 for dinner. Some of the crew, and some of the officers off duty topside, were tasting leftovers on and off all day. I'm happy to say that nobody allowed their alcohol to get the better part of them. Most of the old timers had spent Christmas day aboard ship before, and didn't make a big deal about it, but a few members of the crew had never before experienced being away from loved ones and friends on this the most special holiday of the year.

Things finally went back to routine. I didn't bother to go to the crew's lounge at 19:00 to watch *Alfie* since I had seen it before. Michael Caine and Shelley Winters did superb performances, but not enough to sit through the movie a second time, especially after such a busy day.

◆   ◆   ◆

After the movie, Charlie and I met in Jesse's room. We talked mostly about the East Coast and the places we had just visited on the voyage. K.O. dropped by and like Charlie and myself only drank beer. Jesse quenched his thirst with scotch. We had all enjoyed the voyage, but could hardly wait for the next voyage, especially K.O. I was to learn later that he was really hung up on Asian women. Jesse on the other hand had a fancy for African women of mixed race. That explained his many trips on ships from New Orleans to Capetown and other ports in South Africa during the early and mid-1960's.

To each his own I thought as I listened to their sea stories. Charlie always had some true tales of adventure. We sat in Jesse's room until just after midnight when we all realized that Christmas was long gone and it was time to retire for the night. Before retiring, I went back to the Saloon Mess to check out the situation. Everything was all in place. The night lunch plate was full of leftover pie, fruit, candies, and nuts. Seemingly, a Merry Christmas had been had by all.

The next day the crew prepared to enter port, especially the Deck and Engine Departments. We had only been away for six weeks, but it seemed much longer. The Statue of Liberty looked mighty good from a distance as we sailed into the harbor of Bayonne, New Jersey just after 10:00 on December 27, 1966. The payoff would be at 13:00, conveniently, right after lunch. I would have a busy afternoon getting to the bank, to the Post Office to send money back to San Francisco, and then back to the ship in time to serve dinner.

◆   ◆   ◆

Bayonne became my second home when I did 20 months of my Navy enlistment there in early 1952. Nostalgia hit me when I found myself there again. I was part of the ship's company when there was a supply corps school on base. I was in the process of conversion from Baptist to Catholicism. One of the civilian base workers introduced me to Father Dominic Del Monte, head of Our Lady of Assumption Church on 23rd Street. I had taken instructions earlier at Great Lakes. "Father D," as he was fondly called by some parishioners, sat with me once a week until July when I was baptized. I had just missed confirmation which was every two years, when he and one of his lay assistants took me to Mt. Carmel Church in Jersey City where I was confirmed. We kept in touch even after I was transferred in October 1953.

I chatted sometimes with his secretary, Mrs. Di Angelo, while I was waiting to see him. She was always friendly, but struck me as the type of lady you would not want to be on the wrong side of. She was a no nonsense type. This was an Italian parish. I went to Mass there a number of times and was invited to some of their gatherings. Some of the parishioners were Italian born. Father D would occasionally remind them that I was the fourth African American he had baptized into the faith. The African American community in Bayonne was small in those days, but we had many good times mingling around 21st Street. I went in feeling like an outsider, but from my own people or from these parishioners at Our Lady of Assumption I never experienced a hint of rejection.

After leaving Bayonne I kept in touch for a while. I even wrote cards and letters to Father D and Mrs. Di Angelo from France, Italy, and Portugal while on a world cruise in 1954. After I moved to the West Coast we fell out of touch. On this trip I was in Bayonne only two days and I missed my chance again to get in touch with them. The first day in port I worked overtime to help take on some emergency stores. The short time I did get off the ship I used to pay a visit to an ailing cousin in New York's Harlem. The following day we sailed to Norfolk, Virginia. I promised myself that on my next visit to Bayonne I would make it my first order of business to check on Father D.

◆   ◆   ◆

It was New Year's Eve, 1966, and I thanked my lucky stars we would not be at sea on another major holiday. We would be in port from Saturday through Monday, a brief spell to get our feet back on the ground. It had been four years since my last visit to Norfolk, so I wanted to go ashore for curiosity's sake. I was determined to see how much had changed and how much remained the same since I left there in 1962.

Instead of going on my fact finding tour immediately, I decided to accept an old friend's invitation to a New Year's Eve dinner party. It was on Park Avenue near Brambleton, across the street from present-day Norfolk State University. I went alone after finishing my shipboard duties. At first it was a low-keyed party hosted by my friend Dean and his lovely lady friend, Joyce. But at toward 10:00 PM things got lively. There were about 20 guests. Dean's large dwelling accommodated them easily. There was a variety of alcoholic beverages available and good dance music. The guests ranged from ordinary housewives, to school teachers, doctors, and lawyers. The dinner was served at midnight. It was a feast worth waiting for. It consisted of baked ham, Yankee pot roast, collard greens, potato salad, yams, cornbread, and, of course, black-eyed peas to fulfill the old Southern superstition that eating black-eyed peas on New Year's Eve brings good luck. All the food was laid out buffet style. When I asked Joyce who helped her fix this lay out she shrugged as she pointed to herself. I expressed my compliments as I followed the other guests in loading up my plate. She and Dean were the perfect host and hostess.

I mingled freely with the lady guests but stayed on my best behavior since the vast majority of them had husbands or boyfriends in tow. After pigging myself on the food, I excused myself from the party, returning to the ship at Navy Supply. Most of the other guests were off for New Year's Day and could dance the night away. I, however, had to be at work by 06:30.

As I asked Dean to call my taxi, a couple who were getting ready to leave offered to give me a ride back to the ship. I could hardly believe my luck. This couple lived in Lambert's Point, but did not mind driving me the rest of the way. I owed them many thanks. They refused to accept any compensation. One of the Marines at the gate got me a ride to the ship. That way I was able to get out of the chill.

◆   ◆   ◆

New Year's Day onboard ship was nothing like Christmas. We wished each other a Happy New Year as we met in the passageways and Mess Halls. Although we had a holiday meal many of the crew went ashore, taking advantage of being in port, especially those in the Deck and Engine Departments. The Steward Department worked as usual, but with overtime pay for the holiday. My drinking buddies decided to stay aboard New Year's Night and so did I. I really didn't feel up to the long haul downtown. At around 19:00 I ventured to the Enlisted Men's Club then changed my mind and returned to the ship. I joined several shipmates for a beer then went to bed.

♦   ♦   ♦

On Monday night when I finally went ashore for my fact finding tour, I noticed Norfolk's transition from segregation to integration. I must give credit where credit is due. They had gone through the transition much smoother than the deep South States. When I left four years earlier, segregation was alive and well except token integration into White schools, on buses, and a few other public accommodations. Lunch counters had integrated before I left, but movies, hotels, and restaurants in most cases were still "No-No's." Now in January 1967 I went out on the town sampling hospitality from Church Street to Main to Granby without a hitch. I even went briefly to Ocean View, but was unmoved by the atmosphere.

My friend Dean had already told me about some of the changes in the old neighborhood. He and another friend, Mr. Bernard, told me that servicemen were being treated with more respect.

I visited a bar off Monticello Avenue and sat for a beer. I hoped if I sat in there long enough I would run into a lady named Charlene Anderson.

"Charlie" was a former Navy girl or "WAVE" as they called them in those days. She was from Michigan, but married a sailor and settled down in Norfolk after her hitch in the Navy was finished. Her husband Bill went on to retire from the Navy then became a long-haul truck driver. Charlie was quite happy to be a regular housewife; she was there when Bill needed her. She had a pet project. Being an excellent cook, she would cook dinners at home and bring them to the bars around Norfolk. Word got around fast about her mouth-watering cuisine especially her chicken and pot roast dinners. I met her at a bus stop at Monticello and Brambleton Avenues, just before leaving Norfolk in 1962. She gave me a friendly wave as she drove by. A young man who was also waiting for the bus told me about her dinners. The light changed to red and I ran to the corner before it changed again. I asked her if she had anymore dinners. It just so happened she had one chicken dinner left. She pulled around and parked in front of the Greyhound Bus Station. Due to the taxis and other traffic our transaction had to be brief. I grabbed the chicken dinner and handed her $2.50. The 50 cent tip was all I could afford in those days, especially between pay days. What a bargain! Two pieces of chicken, lettuce and tomato, greens and yams topped off with a small helping of peach cobbler. She told me she dropped by the *Koret* bar once in a while, but otherwise seldom visited Church Street. I gave her Dean's number. She thanked me and drove off. I took my dinner in the bus station, grabbed a

Coke and chowed down. Charlie may have been White, but when it came to cooking, no Soul cook ever stood taller. I would see her two more times for chicken dinners, before leaving for the West Coast.

One of the customers at the bar near Monticello told me she might be in later because the bartender had ordered a dinner. As she walked in the door, she remembered me from four years earlier and we embraced. She handed the bartender his dinner of ham, potato salad, and greens. I told her I was on my way back to the ship. She had four chicken dinners in the car to deliver to some sailors and their girlfriends and she would give me a lift back to the ship. On our way down Hampton Boulevard past Old Dominion University, I noticed the new buildings. It was a whole different landscape. We talked about how happy we were to see each other again after such a long lapse of time. Soon I was getting out of her car at the gate with dinner in hand. We promised to keep in touch as she drove on to the *Tausig* bar to deliver her meals. In a few days Bill would be back off the road and the dinner deliveries would halt. Customers understood Charlie was a White, middle-class housewife first and Soul cook second.

◆   ◆   ◆

The next day we made the short voyage to Charleston. The high point of this trip would be visiting my brother, McPhail and his family. The last time we saw each other was seven years ago at our mother's funeral.

This was a joyous visit. Mac had worked on the railroads in Tennessee and Florida for many years. When he retired to Charleston he met and married his third wife. She had seven children when they married. I spent the night at my brother's home and met his wife and children for the first time. What emotional embraces and meetings. My shipmate Charlie covered breakfast for me so I was able to spend half the day with Mac and his family. I told him to convey my regards to other relatives in Darlington with promises I would see them on another trip east. So much for my short 20 hours in historic Charleston. Next stop Mobile, Alabama.

◆   ◆   ◆

Our stay in Mobile was also short-lived. After all, the Chief Steward had already admonished us not to forget that the ship's bosses, mainly the U.S. government, had one thing in mind, to get the ship loaded as quickly as possible for the voyage to eastern Asia and Vietnam. Many in the crew didn't seem to realize that. They believed that the ship should stay longer in certain ports that they enjoyed. Quite a few of the crew really enjoyed Mobile. They roamed from one section of the city to the other in search of wine, women, and song. Like most seaports in the Gulf States, Mobile had little trouble supplying either. The same would happen in New Orleans a few nights later.

7

NEW ORLEANS

This was my first visit to New Orleans. I found it to be a cultural world different from other Gulf port cities. At the time of our visit, mid-January 1967, the signs reading "Whites Only" were all down, as in most other parts of the South, but the city was still in no hurry to abandon its old habits of accepting people not as they are but judging on skin color alone.

I decided to go out on the town with Bruce, Jesse, and Charlie. We skipped dinner onboard ship and headed for some Soul eatery for a home cooked meal. Bruce had visited New Orleans before and took us to a restaurant where he knew the owner. Danielle was a fairly large-sized lady with a charming smile. Bruce embraced her like a long lost friend then turned and introduced each of us by first names.

"I would like for you to meet my friend of seven years, Danielle, better known to me as Danni," he said.

"Pleased to meet you," was our immediate reply.

Danni led us to an empty table near the back. The restaurant was filling up fast. The aroma from the kitchen spoke for itself. There was no doubt we were in an eating establishment that was Soul all the way. I could hardly wait to see the menu. As I was glancing at it, I told Bruce how good it would be to try some shrimp gumbo.

"Be cool," he ordered, "Danni is fixing us up really nice."

Danni reappeared along with one of her waitresses. They were bringing a family style dinner we would serve ourselves. "This is all on her," Bruce assured us.

Like it or not they brought us all shrimp gumbo and rice in four individual bowls and a tossed salad in a large bowl. The salad and gumbo were followed by macaroni and cheese, green beans, and cornbread. It looked like we were ready to chow down!

"Help yourselves," Danni insisted as she returned to the kitchen.

She didn't have to worry; we were already doing just that. Bruce and Danni were really close friends. He and some shipmates would show up at her restaurant on each visit to New Orleans with gifts and souvenirs from various ports around the world. Bruce held her in very high esteem, rightfully so.

We finally finished our main course and the waitress came back with homemade pound cake a la mode for dessert. This was no greasy spoon. It lived up to its name: *Danni's Best*. My shipmates agreed that no place in Storyville could be much better. Customers kept coming in until the place was just about full. We finally finished our dessert. The attractive waitress was very attentive. Out of curiosity I asked her name. She said it was Claudette. Since dinner was free, each of us dropped five dollars on Claudette's tray. She gasped saying she hadn't received a tip that large in years. She laughed almost uncontrollably. Her excitement brought a curious stare from nearby customers and envious glares from her coworkers. After all, she had a reason to be excited. *Danni's Best* was by no means exclusive. Its clientele was made up mostly of lower income people who could not afford such handsome tips. Claudette told us to come again soon.

"Thanks again!" we told Danni for her hospitality.

We decided to hit the clubs and other joints on a trial and error basis. We split up with Bruce and Charlie staying behind to visit with Danni and Claudette until closing time. Bruce had given Jesse the next day off, so he headed off to Plaquemine to visit with friends and relatives.

Jesse had gone far since he started shipping a number of years earlier. He bought a home in Hempstead, Long Island, New York after meeting and marrying a girl from South Africa. In spite of these accomplishments, he never forgot where he came from; that is, the state of Louisiana. In spite of his drunken behavior at times, we would become close friends.

Now it was time for me to take in the sights of New Orleans on my own, at least some of them. I took a taxi to Canal Street then inside the French Quarter to Bourbon Street. I was keenly aware of the Civil Rights Act of 1964 that barred discrimination in public establishments. Some of the White establishments still maintained the "where there's a will, there's a way" attitude when it came to delaying what they saw as the onslaught of forced integration. Like other places in the South, and a number of places in the North also, they would go private rather than integrate. The owners of bars, clubs, and restaurants would often require membership or rather showing of a membership card to be a customer in a particular establishment. We Blacks learned from some of our White shipmates that while Blacks were denied entry due to a lack of membership, some Whites walked right in without even being asked to show any membership identification.

These incidents also took place in Mobile. No hard feelings, but out of curiosity I would have to see for myself. I went to several clubs on Canal Street, but was turned away for lack of membership. Since I didn't consider myself a trouble-maker I kept telling myself that being turned away from these clubs had nothing to do with race. Now it was time to take a stroll to Bourbon Street.

On my way there I met an attractive young woman of color. She was friendly and wanted to know what I was doing in those parts. I told her I was out for a night on the town. She said her name was Adrian. I told her to call me Buzz. She had a friendly smile on her face, but I assumed she was a streetwalker all the way. I was truthful to her when I told her about being on the ship and out on the town. She was happy to oblige when I asked her to show me a bar or club where we could get in without a hassle. She knew her way around.

When we entered this bar on Bourbon Street, the bouncer surprisingly greeted us with a smile. We spent about an hour there getting better acquainted. It was a cool atmosphere. The predominantly White audience was very much in order.

"Buzz getting a buzz?" Adrian said as she sipped her gin and tonic.

"Yes," I said as I sipped bourbon and 7-Up.

"Buzz drinking bourbon on Bourbon Street."

We both laughed at that one. Adrian then lectured me on being careful, telling me to avoid certain sections of town. I thanked her for the advice. It was time to use a little psychology since she told me about her own neighborhood being a little rough at times. She lived in suburban Gretna. If she was so willing to warn me about these bad places, I in turn was willing to trust her more as the night wore on. I suggested to her that we go to the Treme neighborhood where I was earlier. Just about everything and everybody there was Soul all the way.

We taxied there and entered *The Desire* bar. It was really jumping. A middle-aged lady was wailing on a low down Blues number backed by a small band. It was nearly midnight but I didn't care. I told Adrian that I didn't have to be back aboard ship until noon because of stores coming aboard. She giggled and then told me how envious she was of me for having so much time off. She had to be at work by 7:00 AM at a downtown cafeteria.

"Lay off a day," I said half joking.

"No, no!" was her reply.

She was saving up enough money to move into an apartment. As it was, she was living with her parents in a home with four bedrooms. She occupied one of the rooms which had a separate entrance from the street. She hit me like a ton of bricks when she told me how she enjoyed her days off, but would sometimes sac-rifice one of them by dropping by an employment agency that would give a day's work of casual labor. She had just worked such a job two days earlier. She was happy to get the job, although it was only for four hours, at a restaurant. In fact, when we met off Canal Street she had just left a restaurant where she had filled in a few times, but nothing was available. The band was getting down on a really soulful Jazz tune while Adrian was running all this down to me. She then continued after I asked her some personal questions.

"How old are you?" I asked.

She answered without hesitation that she was 22.

"You look a little younger," I assured her.

"Thank you," she replied.

Then I wanted to know more about her. She volunteered some more information telling about her failed marriage beginning when she was 18 and lasting only two years at which time she had to cut him loose because of his abusive and alcoholic behavior. She couldn't put up with him any longer especially after he struck her.

"I had to leave him," she said in a low tone. "He struck me, something I never saw my father do to my mother. If I stayed with him one of us would be dead by now."

She had a three year old son. Her mother and retired maternal grandmother helped her take care of him. She paid them just as she would any babysitter who might happen to be a non-relative.

She declined another drink and so did I. Although the bar was staying open all night, like so many other bars and clubs in New Orleans, we both had obligations to meet in just a few hours. She had only two drinks while I had three. She was very much in charge of herself. Then I asked her whether she could put me up for the night. She hesitated then told me that I looked and acted like a real gentleman. I thanked her for the compliment. She told me I could stay at her place providing I was willing to rise at 6:00 AM. She would normally rise at 5:30 on work days. It sounded good to me. With that agreement we were on our way to Gretna by way of taxi.

◆   ◆   ◆

Adrian was a good housekeeper. In her spacious room everything was arranged right in place, neat and clean. This duplex dwelling gave her not only her own private entrance, but a private bath and kitchenette as well. I asked her for a glass of cold water which she thought was a good idea. She poured one for herself as well. The clock on the dresser reminded us both of how late it was; almost 2:00

AM. I thanked her again for letting me stay at her place so I wouldn't have to sleep back aboard ship. Smiling, she said she trusted me as she sat on her son's made up bed. He would be spending the night next door with her parents and teenaged sister. She also had a brother just a year younger than she was, living in Slidell.

Without hardly any further preliminaries, we were in bed amid each other's warm embraces and kisses. I had left my clothes on the large single chair I had been sitting on earlier. The bourbon made me forget something I would surely remember a few hours later...

The coffee aroma awoke me at around 5:50 AM. Adrian had already gotten up, showered, and made coffee. Her built in alarm clock was working like a charm. I rushed in the bathroom to take a five minute shower. She had some perfumed soap. The lukewarm water really felt good. I grabbed an extra towel from the rack and as I dried off I thought of something. I rushed back into the room and grabbed my trousers looking into the front pockets. Everything was still there, just as I left it four hours earlier. I quickly dressed while taking sips of orange juice. I had suddenly thought of other plans for Adrian and me. We would take a taxi to her job and have breakfast at the cafeteria, taking my own sweet time. She said she was grateful for my generosity, but that would be too expensive. I had already shown my kindness by allowing her to show me the town and getting her home in a taxi, she had a better idea. She was going to work in a carpool and would be sure they could squeeze me in.

"Let's go out front they'll be along in less than ten minutes."

We went out front and there they were, already waiting. Adrian introduced me.

◆   ◆   ◆

I could see the *Crescent City* ahead in the semi-darkness. Before I could strike a casual conversation, we were pulling up at the cafeteria and going in the door. Adrian told me to sit down and she would be right back. She was going to see her boss. I guess she told him I was going to have breakfast. A few minutes later she came through the line with a tray of food including hot cakes, scrambled eggs, crisp bacon, hash brown potatoes and a glass of orange juice. The friendly faced White lady at the cash register waved her right on by. When she came to the table and set the tray in front of me I hardly knew what to say.

"Enjoy your breakfast," she said.

Adrian said she would be back later to sit with me a few minutes. First she had to go back in the kitchen to help out the prep cooks. Later she would be back on the line with the other attractive young ladies. Adrian's boss, the cafeteria manager, came by my table. He was a clean cut White guy in his late twenties. He asked if I were from New Orleans.

"No, I was born in South Carolina," I told him, "but I haven't lived there in nearly 20 years."

Then I told him about my job on the ship and that we were in New Orleans picking up Military cargo.

"They call me Buzz," I offered.

"Steve," he said.

As we shook hands, he wished me a safe trip. After Steve left the table, I proceeded to finish my lumberjack breakfast. I went over to the water fountain and brought back a tall glass to wash it down. A young Soul brother passed by with a bus cart. He asked me if I were enjoying my meal. I assured him I was. Without asking, he went to the fountain and brought me another glass of water. I thanked him and handed him a dollar. He was surprised. After thanking me he told me customers seldom tipped him. I could tell by our short conversation that he was educated. I asked him if he were enrolled at one of the local colleges or universities. It turned out he was in his junior year at Dillard University majoring in Political Science. His fair skin gave him away as being of mixed race. One would have to look close at him to tell he was a Soul brother. I wouldn't have dared ask him about his obvious mixed racial background as I considered it too personal a question. His name was Breaux and he was juggling his work and school schedules quite well. His job at the cafeteria was only part time. I told him how I would like to visit some of the many universities and cultural centers in New Orleans, especially the predominately Black ones like Xavier University. He said it would be cool. Some of his friends were enrolled at Xavier. He would be happy to show me around if I ever visited Dillard. I told him it would have to be another time because the ship was sailing the next day.

"I wish I were taking off with you guys to share some of that overseas adventure," he said with an excited look on his face. I offered him some advice.

"Stay and get your education first, then go for adventure later," I told him. "Time is on your side." I thanked him for his hospitality.

"My pleasure," he said. "Remember, I'm Breaux and come back to see us on your next trip."

Then he went on to cover his job cleaning the tables after the morning rush. As I sat alone trying to recover from that hearty breakfast, I slowly sipped my second glass of water. Then a terrible guilt enveloped me as my thoughts went back to Adrian. I thought about when we had first met the night before. Here was this lovely young lady with this charming smile befriending me, yet I was silently branding her as a streetwalker. Remembering our visits to the clubs, I knew I got more of a buzz on than she did. She caringly warned me about dangers around the city, took me into her home, shared a bed with me, and never asked me for a penny. Nor did she take a penny from my pockets when she had the chance. The average streetwalker or tramp would hardly pass up the opportunity to help themselves to the two hundred dollars I had in my pocket. Adrian was an independent woman, too proud to free load off her parents or to accept any kind of public assistance. She worked her way. Yes, I really felt guilty about this sexual stereotyping of a nice person. Somehow I would have to make it up to her. I had just come up with an idea and was deep in thought when Adrian reappeared at the table.

"Hey there, don't go to sleep on me," she said.

"No, I won't," I replied

She said she would be going on her lunch break in a half an hour and apologized for not being able to come back out sooner. I understood. Time had moved faster than I had realized. It was already 10:30 AM. I had had some company to pass the time away. Another young woman came from behind the line to chat briefly after the morning rush. She introduced herself as Dottie. She had been playing peek-a-boo all morning. It was nice chatting with her. Breaux came back several more times, once with a glass of punch for me. He pretended to be wiping tables around where I was sitting, but was really asking me about California and telling me how he would like to get there one day. I told him again that time was on his side but when he does make it out that way he should try to take in the whole West Coast by traveling north through Oregon and Washington. He was impressed. Breaux pushed his bus cart away, preparing the cafeteria for the noon hour. There were a number of banks and office buildings in the area and their lunch rush would begin in about an hour.

I was off for the day but I had promised Bruce I would help him and K.O. arrange some stores. After all, I could always use the overtime.

Adrian came back to the table and asked me to stay and have lunch with her. Dottie and one of the Soul cooks would join us. It was their break time also. Larry, the cook, told me what was on the lunch menu. When he said red beans and rice, I told him to stop right there. My choice would be a bowl of beef stew with a side of red beans and rice. Being treated to three free meals in a row and meeting all kinds of nice people, I figured this could only happen in New Orleans.

Larry returned with the food. He brought me an extra treat of yellow corn bread and some punch. The four of us sat down to lunch. They were munching, but I was pigging out in a big way. Then I came up with a suggestion. I had spent four hours at the downtown cafeteria. I would have to return to the ship for about three hours. I turned to Adrian asking her if we could meet somewhere about 5:00 PM or a little later. I was hoping it would be at Adrian's place in Gretna, maybe I could meet her family. Before Adrian could answer, Larry spoke up telling me he had a car and they could pick me up at the Army pier or wherever the ship was docked.

"Sounds okay to me," Dottie said.

Adrian was for it too. We all reminded each other that we could not make a late night out of it because of our early work shifts the next day. We had something in common; we all had jobs in food service.

Just as their break was about over, Breaux came back to the table. He had taken off his apron and white cap. He was off for the day and making it to his 2:00 PM class. Adrian asked him to drive me back to the ship on his way to class. He said he'd be glad to do me the favor.

"Girl, I'm getting more and more in debt to you," I said.

I got up and gave her a bear hug and a kiss on the cheek. She looked so lovely even in her work clothes. I gave Larry the directions to the ship and told them I would meet them at the gate.

"Don't be late," Dottie cautioned with a laugh. I assured them all that I would be right there waiting.

On our way out of the cafeteria, I spotted Steve talking to the lady at the cash register. He told me to come again as the clerk wished me a safe trip. I thanked them both for their hospitality; after all I had spent nearly half a day in their place of business. I waved at the two Soul sisters on the line. Both of them returned my greeting in a very friendly way.

◆   ◆   ◆

Breaux's late model Chevy was in good shape. He drove me around town to see some of the laced-iron balconies, old French mansions, and other charming, old-world sights. There was so much to see that a person could never see it all in one day. As we headed in the direction of the ship, I told him how lucky he was to have been born and brought up in New Orleans, a city of so many diverse cultures. He banged the steering wheel as he laughed and then spoke a few words of French. I guessed that it was his Creole background talking. He said he wanted to get out of the city for awhile when he finished college. Maybe it was just another "young and the restless" attitude. He was only 21. When he let me out at the gate I told him to say hello to his lady friend for me.

"By all means," he said, adding that he would like for me to meet her on my next trip through.

I told him I could hardly wait as I slipped him a ten dollar bill. I noticed the surprised look on his face, while telling me he had given me a lift to the ship as a favor, not for money.

"Take it for gas," I insisted as I shoved it into his hand. He said he could use it and thanked me, giving me a firm handshake. For a part-time bus person in those days, I had just handed him more than a day's pay.

◆   ◆   ◆

I went aboard and reported to the Chief Steward. Bruce told me he had changed his mind about working in the storeroom. We would do it the next day when we were at sea, instead. That was alright with me. At 12:30, it was quiet aboard ship and I went to my room and crashed for a couple of hours. Charlie and most of the crew in the Deck and Engine Departments who weren't on duty were ashore. Jesse had not yet returned from Plaquemine. Many of the officers up topside were still ashore too.

It was just about 16:00 when I jumped up from my afternoon nap, got a quick clean-up, and changed my clothing. Then I was on my way to the gate.

◆   ◆   ◆

My timing couldn't have been better. About ten minutes later my new-found friends drove up. All three had changed. Larry and Dottie were up front as I took the back seat with Adrian. I caught the aroma of both ladies' fresh and perfumed bodies. We were in for a nice evening. I intended to enjoy myself because my party was slowly coming to an end. The next morning aboard ship I would be called out at 06:00.

Larry laid out the scenario of the evening. We would get in two, whirlwind tours to the campuses of Dillard and Xavier. Both campuses looked awesome. Some of those gray stone buildings looked as though they had been standing for a hundred years. Students around us were holding hands, chatting in groups, or making their way to various classes or the library. Both universities were living examples of African American culture in an educational setting.

Since night was approaching, I declined a visit to the historic cemetery. A visit there would be better appreciated in the daylight. I would also pass up visits to the predominately White universities like Tulane and the University of New Orleans until another visit to the city. As we drove through the neighborhoods, I noticed some of them were mixed, with Whites and Blacks living next door to each other. Larry, who was in his late thirties, said that it had been going on ever since he could remember. I had also noticed those kinds of neighborhoods in Charleston. I drew the conclusion that it was a carry over from antebellum days. As a visitor in New Orleans, one can't help noticing that there are some parts of the city that look just as they did when the French and Spanish were running the show there many moons ago.

"So much for the grand tour of the city," I said.

I told them I wanted to save some for my next visit. It was 7:00 PM and time for dinner. I asked them if they had been to Danni's restaurant. They all said yes. I told them dinner would be on me. Off we went. Upon arrival, I was happy to see we found a table right away. Before we could order I saw the boss. She came over and greeted us. I introduced Larry, Dottie, and Adrian. Then Bruce walked up to the table. He was also introduced. Danni told me that for a person who never visited New Orleans before, I sure meet people fast.

Dottie sounded the keynote saying, "Yes, he spent half the day with us at our job. We love him."

We checked out the menu and agreed on the same a la carte meal: fried chicken, mashed potatoes, and green beans. The waitress was very friendly but I asked right away about Claudette. I learned she had the night off. This waitress' name was Wilma.

The four of us engaged in small talk as we ate from the over-filled plates Wilma brought from the kitchen. The gravy over the mashed potatoes was a very dark brown. The soup was yellow split pea. Dottie had begun to show her real self. She was sitting next to Larry, right across from Adrian, when she became quite loud. I could tell by the smell of her breath she had sampled some alcohol after work. She was yelling across the restaurant at people she recognized. It hardly did any good when Larry told her to shut up. She was 30 years old, but acted like she was a spoiled teenager. Dottie was eight years Adrian's senior, but Adrian acted so much more intelligently. Neither Adrian nor I had any intention of interfering. Dottie was just letting her hair down after a full day's work. Bruce and Danni were sitting at a nearby table taking it all in. Both were wearing smirks on their faces and occasionally shaking their heads. As we finished our apple pie a la mode and washed it down with grape punch, I asked Wilma for the check. She just smiled and said it was all taken care of. Danni had done it again. All in all I had four free meals in a row, all paid for by my new-found friends. Surely I could make it up to them somehow. I briefly excused myself from the table and went over to where Bruce and Danni were sitting.

"I owe you two," I told Danni, thanking her for her gracious hospitality.

"No you don't," she said.

All she wanted was a small souvenir from overseas. Bruce butted in by saying that he would see that I do just that. Then I said so long to Danni and told Bruce I would see him tomorrow back aboard the ship. He warned me not to get lost. I assured him that would never happen again like it did in Sydney.

The four of us got up to leave and I placed a five dollar tip on the table for Wilma. She thanked me and told me I'd better come back to see her. I thanked her for the hospitality and soon we were out of the door.

All three of my companions were thanking me for the meal. I told them the pleasure was all mine, then asked them to consider going over to *The Desire* for a few rounds of drinks.

"Hell yes! Wash some of that dinner down," said Dottie. "I feel like a pregnant cow."

Adrian agreed and so did Larry, reminding me he had to rise at 4:30 the next morning. Adrian was the lucky one; she had the next day off.

◆   ◆   ◆

The crowd at *The Desire* was upbeat and so was the music. I had heard so much about some of the places in that particular neighborhood, I expected just about anything. The bouncers and other people in authority were maintaining a strictly no nonsense attitude, expecting their patrons to have a good time but not to rock the boat.

It was the usual gin fizz for Adrian, scotch and water for Larry, and bourbon for me. Dottie however, ordered a double scotch on the rocks.

"I'll be dammed," was all Larry could say.

Adrian and I laughed. By the time we had the next round of drinks, Dottie was feeling no pain. Her double scotches were catching up fast. As I escorted her onto the dance floor, she was fighting for balance. I danced the next number with Adrian. Larry sat that one out, choosing to stay at the table with Dottie. We had one more round and Dottie was really carrying on.

"Play that Black ass music!" she shouted. "I love it. I love all of you Black ass people! That's what it's all about!"

The men at the next table started snickering while their ladies looked on in disgust. Dottie was in no condition to care. She was throwing up her hands and singing along with the music. She even went back on the dance floor and danced by herself. The bouncer didn't interfere. He realized she was only making a fool out of herself, not causing any major trouble for the club.

Larry and Dottie were close friends, having worked together at the cafeteria for a number of years. Before she returned to the table, Larry told me Dottie's husband had recently walked out on her and their three kids. She and the children moved in with an older sister in Gretna. Larry said that as embarrassing as her drunken behavior is, she means well. Larry had a wife and four children at home himself. He was instrumental in helping Dottie catch up with her husband to get child support. Adrian sat through his tale without commenting. I could understand her reaction judging from what she had told me about her own failed marriage. She seemed to have been coping with the situation a bit better than Dottie. When Dottie returned to the table we all agreed it was time to go. Larry called the shots since he was driving.

I wouldn't be able to stay over with Adrian. For her day off, she had plans to spend the night with her family. All of them, including her son, would have breakfast together. She would later take her son out to the park. With the weekend approaching, I would love to have been there to go out with her on her day off and meet her family but it was just not to be. Not this trip anyway.

Larry suggested he drive us to Gretna and leave me at Adrian's place while he saw Dottie home. He would then come back to Adrian's to pick me up and drive me back to the ship. I told him that would be a lot of driving around for a person who had to be up at 4:30 AM. He told me not to worry about it he only lived about two miles from where the ship was docked. We finished our drinks and were on our way to Gretna.

As we drove to Adrian's place Dottie was singing and laughing about how she would love to have someone who needed her. I tried to console her from the backseat by telling her we all needed her.

"We need each other. We've all got our troubles, but there are others who have theirs too."

"Thank you sweetie," she replied. "You're so nice."

"It's good she's off tomorrow," Adrian whispered.

I told her I was happy for both of them for having the day off. I suggested she take her son shopping. She said that shopping would have to wait until next payday.

As Larry dropped us off, I went around to Dottie's side of the car and told her to be strong for her children's sake and that I would be in touch with her. With that I gave her a kiss on the cheek.

"Thank you," she responded feebly.

◆   ◆   ◆

It was not quite 11:00 PM as Adrian and I relaxed briefly in her place. I had read between the lines, sensing that Larry would give us time to talk and be together a while. I told her how nice she had been to me; hosting me both in her home and on her job. As we sat on the sofa, I told her it was payback time. She said that she really didn't look at it that way. She said she took a liking to me. Ordinarily she doesn't pick up strangers and bring them into her home. I thanked her for making me an exception, reached into my pocket and pulled out all the money I had brought ashore. I counted out 80 dollars and laid it on her coffee table. I told her to take her son to a movie or buy him something nice rather than waiting for payday.

She sat there speechless through the whole conversation. When she finally got her composure, she said, she didn't know how to accept the money. I told her I insisted. Her friends didn't have to know. It would be our little secret. I also told her to enjoy both of her days off that week. No casual labor visits. She said she had already saved enough to make a security deposit on a larger apartment and she would do just that.

"Thank you," I said as I gave her a big hug and a few kisses on the lips.

I told her I would like to write to her and she gave me her address then added her phone number. As she handed it to me her hands shook a little. She asked me why I was so nice. I told her I tried to be nice because I had met a nice person in her and I had met some nice people through her. The conversation turned to Dottie. I told Adrian maybe I would send Dottie something through her. She said that would be nice, but she could give me her address if I wanted it. I politely declined saying I would rather write to Dottie through her. She insisted I write her on my own. We laughed at each other for arguing over correspondence. She finally won out by giving me Dottie's address. I in turn told her how concerned I was about Dottie's excessive drinking. So was she, but she thought Dottie would eventually turn herself around. She was already drinking less now than she had been right after her husband took off. I took note of one encouraging thing Adrian said which was that Dottie hardly ever missed a day at work. She was quite dependable. Adrian then asked if she could get me something. I was still full from dinner and drinking but I accepted a cold glass of water from her. I noticed that the South was its same old self in the respect of feeding and entertaining their guests. They would put food and drink on the table and invite you to help yourself. Often it didn't matter whether the host or hostess was of wealth and privilege or of humble background. This hospitality quite often didn't exist in the North.

We continued chatting until Larry knocked on the door. Adrian let him in. She had already reluctantly accepted the money and stashed it away out of sight. Larry refused Adrian's offer of any refreshments saying he had to get home before his wife sent a posse out searching for him. We all laughed together.

The three of us walked out to the car. I turned to Adrian and told her to remember what I told her about taking both of her days off and enjoying a good rest while spending more time with her son.

"Oh yes, I will," she promised.

She wanted me to meet her family on the next visit. It sounded good. We embraced and kissed goodbye. Then I jumped in the car. Larry waved and told her to enjoy her day off. We watched her go into her parent's home then drove off. I felt relieved to know that she would not be spending the night all alone.

◆   ◆   ◆

On the way back to the ship I again thanked Larry for the hospitality all of them had shown me during my short stay in New Orleans. He in turn thanked me for the dinner and drinks. He told me he would like to have me visit his home for dinner on one of my next visits to New Orleans. He was sure his wife and family would love to meet me. It gave me a warm feeling to be receiving such a welcome, even as a stranger.

Before long we had reached the ship. Larry asked me to wait a few seconds while he wrote down his address and telephone number and told me to get in touch with him on my next trip to town. As I got out of the car I told him to get home safe. Then I handed him a 20 dollar bill. At first he refused to accept it saying he did me these favors as a friend. In explaining my point of view, I reminded him of all the trips back and forth to Gretna, the sightseeing tour of the city, as well as getting me back to the ship. I told him that his almost new Ford was burning gas and gas cost money. That is where my 20 dollar gift would come in.

"Thanks man," he said grudgingly as he accepted the money.

"Have a safe voyage."

"I'll try," was my answer.

He then reached out the window and gave me a firm handshake. As Larry drove off I could tell that in spite of three rounds of scotch at *The Desire*, he was very much in charge of his driving.

◆   ◆   ◆

After showing my identification, I went inside the gate and back aboard the ship. The sailing board read: "Panama Canal Zone." For the time being my party was over. Getting five hours of sleep before my duty call would be a big help. Both the Galley and Mess Halls would be wide open come morning. The ship would be sailing just a few hours after breakfast.

I had all the tables set, but some of the non-watch standers were a no-show. Charlie and I chatted about our experiences in port as he cleaned out the pantry. He had been to New Orleans many times before and began telling me about some crazy people he had met there over the years. But he always looked forward to coming back. Before breakfast was over I snuck into the Crew Mess to listen to the exchange of sea stories. Most of the crew members were talking at the same time. They talked about the women, the rip-offs, and the clubs. I decided to wait until after dinner to tell of my new-found friends and the good times we had.

Charlie finished up in the storeroom and began cutting up spring onions and radishes for lunch. Jesse was in the Galley filling orders. Juan was getting pies ready for lunch. Ken was in the far corner of the Galley peeling potatoes. K.O. was carrying out his usual duties as Chief Cook in the back of the Galley, placing meats he had chopped up for dinner in the chill box and going over some menus with Bruce. As usual, we were very much on top of our jobs.

I returned to the Saloon Mess and began wiping out the breadboxes, clearing the tables, and cleaning the refrigerator. We shared the work well and it was nice to know we would all be together again for the next voyage.

◆   ◆   ◆

Since I wouldn't be setting up for lunch just yet, I went out on deck. We were getting underway. I started to reflect on the city. I thought of some of its great entertainers like Louis Armstrong and Fats Domino. Too bad I couldn't stay for Mardi Gras but duty was calling. Maybe some other time. I thought about the recent football bowl games, both college and professional, but my main thoughts were on the five people I met in New Orleans who I keep referring to as new-found friends. I admired their sense of reality. Those with children would occasionally go out on the town, but would hardly cross the line. When all was said and done they did not shirk their responsibilities to their children. They showed a strong sense of family values. Barring any unforeseen incidents, these people will always be close to me.

They welcomed me not as a stranger, but treated me with face value. That's why I reciprocated in kind with the monetary gifts. I felt like a Black Santa Claus in mid-January.

As I stood on deck leaning over the rail I thought of New Orleans as it is shown in old movie scenes like the slave auctions shown in Clark Gable and Yvonne De Carlo's movie *Band of Angels* and the slave quarters depicted in *A Streetcar Named Desire* starring Marlon Brando and Vivian Leigh.

Suddenly I had to admit that my stay in New Orleans was over. As we pulled away from the dock and began to transit the Mississippi River I faced the facts that I was not some rich tourist who could spend another month or even an extra week in New Orleans, but I was just another seafarer who has to leave when the fog whistle blows.

◆   ◆   ◆

As I went back inside to set the tables for lunch, I thought of the profound effect the East Coast trip had had on me. I reflected on both the places in the North that I had been to many times before like Bayonne, New York; Norfolk and Charleston; and the gulf ports that were new to me, like Mobile and New Orleans. Ending my stay there, I promised to be obedient to the hosts and hostesses I had met who directed me:

"Y'all come back. Y'all hear?

8

SAN FRANCISCO

We went straight through the Canal Zone stopping briefly once we were on the Pacific Ocean side at Rodman Naval Base. I didn't go ashore in Cristobol or Balboa except to go to the Enlisted Men's Club after work. It was my fourth trip through the Canal Zone but I never get tired of watching those locks open and close. The workers make their jobs look like a ritual. The change back to a tropical climate was quite a relief. The short stay in Panama was alright with me. I really had no desire to stay longer, although I made the best of it while I was there.

◆   ◆   ◆

San Francisco in late January was as expected: a mixture of fair skies, rain, fog, and cool weather. Having lived there off and on for more than three years, I had well adapted myself to whatever the weather may bring. We pulled in and docked at Pier 39 under fair skies. We only had an overnight stay there because of a minimum of cargo to load then there would be a shift to the Oakland Army Terminal. Of course I called Betty to suggest we go out to dinner after work. I told her I had not bothered to go by my old neighborhood yet. I changed my mind about dinner since I wouldn't get to her place until 7:00 PM; I would just accept whatever leftovers she had in her fridge. She would hear none of it. She would have dinner ready for me when I arrived. We cut our conversation short since I was calling her at work. I too was on duty and needed to start setting up for lunch.

It's amazing how Betty and I hit it off so well. I met her shortly after returning to the West Coast a few years earlier. We were from two diverse cultures. She was from New York, born in the Harlem Hospital; I was delivered by a midwife on a farm in South Carolina. We did have some important things in common though, we were both children of the Great Depression and we had both swapped the East Coast for the West. Betty made the move when she was in the Army.

◆   ◆   ◆

Just as promised, dinner was ready when I arrived. She had made pork chops all smothered in brown gravy complete with apple sauce, mashed potatoes, and greens. Through dinner we talked about the voyage and I brought her up on the happenings in New York. She hadn't been back there in nearly four years. We talked about my decision to go on another voyage. She reminded me of my plans for school and I assured her I would be in school as a near middle-aged student, come summer. Then the subject was changed. I wanted her to help me entertain some guests from the ship two nights later; at my expense of course. Betty said it would be alright with her as long as it wouldn't last until the wee hours of the morning. I assured her it wouldn't. We finished our ice cream and she quickly washed the dishes. As we were listening to Nancy Wilson records I was truthful about my chance meetings with Judy in Sydney and Adrian in New Orleans. I didn't go into every detail, but she read between the lines. Betty knew she was still number one as far as I was concerned. I told her I didn't want to fall into this "girl in every port" thing. I knew Betty so well. She would always be nothing but a one man's woman. Spending the night with her was always a pleasure whether it was an early rise at 5:30 like the next morning or an 11:00 AM sleep-in like we did a number of times in the past. A good time would still be had.

◆   ◆   ◆

The next morning we took a taxi ride in style from the Avenues to lower Market Street where I dropped her off at her job. I then went back to the ship at Pier 39. Being an early riser, Charlie had the tables all set up. I proceeded to put the finishing touches on them and we both went into the Crew Mess for pastries and coffee.

As usual, the crewmen who had gone ashore last night were telling of their experiences. A few hadn't gotten any further from the ship than Fishermen's Wharf. The majority had ventured into North Beach and the Tenderloin District where the pickings were a bit better. Some told stories of picking up so called "nice girls" until the girl dropped the price on them. Others paid the price asked by the street hustlers rather than leave empty handed. Some of the crew told such weird tales that a lumberjack would have been blushing.

It was soon time to serve breakfast and the faithful and hungry were arriving. Sea watches had been broken. Chief Officer Sullivan came in off deck, grabbed a banana muffin and some coffee, and walked back out. He believed in eating a light breakfast and lunch and a hearty dinner. We exchanged pleasantries before he left, but he was in a hurry to check things out with the Bos'n as well as others in the Deck Department. All seemed to be going well. Bruce had the Steward Department in line and the Engine Department was making ready for our shift to the Oakland Army Terminal pier in two hours. For off-duty shore leave, most of the crew would still come to the San Francisco side, especially those with new-found girlfriends.

Time was of an essence, so most of the crew shared taxis rather than fool around with trans-bay buses.

The crew soon learned something that was music to our ears. The ship would be in Oakland all weekend. Day workers and engine wipers were really happy because they would only have to work if they wanted overtime. As for us in the Steward Department, we were on duty as usual but got paid overtime for Saturday and Sunday. That was alright with me.

◆   ◆   ◆

Saturday night was the party at Betty's place. I was looking forward to playing host. Eight of my shipmates showed up including my drinking buddies Bruce, Charlie and Jesse. All of them brought a girl along. Not surprising since they had been coming to the Bay Area for a number of years. Bob Harris brought his wife. Since he had the next day off, they would be driving home to Hayward after the party. Both of the wipers were there as well as several girls Betty had invited from work. All were ready to party. Jake and Dale, who had not brought girls, immediately latched on to Betty's girlfriends. It didn't seem to matter that the girls were about five years their senior. Within a half an hour the four of them were out the door. They said that they were going to *Jack's Place*, a club on Sutter Street in the middle of the Fillmore District. They wanted to jam awhile. It was obvious my two young shipmates would be their company for the night. Betty looked on as though she didn't believe what she was seeing.

"Carry on!" Bob Harris told them as he laughed out loud. His wife in turn gave him an icy glare. The party was on. I passed the cheese dips around and helped Betty entertain the more than 20 guests. The other food was laid out buffet style. There was plenty of food and drink available. The guests wanted for nothing. I helped myself to some fried chicken and potato salad, but avoided the Chili Mac.

Remembering my duties and obligations would start early the next morning, I only had two glasses of bourbon and 7-Up. The party music was a knockout mix of Blues, Jazz, and Rock. Just about everybody was in the mood for dancing. Betty really hosted a good party. She danced with almost all the guys and told the ladies not to be anti-social. The party had gone on since about 8:00 PM. Some of the guests began to trickle out just before midnight. They all gave Betty many thanks for a really nice party. Bruce, Charlie, and Jesse thanked us both. They had introduced us to their lady friends earlier. Betty told them all to come again. Bob Harris and his wife thanked us again before heading for Hayward. They invited us to visit them sometime. One of Betty's neighbors was kind enough to stay and help scrape and wash the dishes. All we had to do was dance to one more number before getting to bed.

◆   ◆   ◆

Very early Sunday morning I was winding my way back across the bay to serve breakfast aboard ship. It was a bit on the quiet side. I missed out on church because of duties in the Mess but managed to take in an afternoon movie between lunch and dinner. After working dinner, I shared a taxi into San Francisco with Bruce and Charlie. Jesse would party the night away in Oakland where one of his girlfriends lived. Once on San Francisco's upper Market Street we split up and I caught a bus back to Betty's place. Some leftovers from the party were great for dinner as we tuned in first to *The Ed Sullivan Show* and later a made-for-TV movie. It would be an early night for us with a Blue Monday approaching.

On Monday I was able to get over to my old place to pick up some clothing for the next voyage. That evening after serving dinner Betty and I got together again but it would only be for a few hours. No overnight stay tonight, the ship would be sailing the next morning. We talked about things like keeping in touch and she declined my offer to help pay for the party. She said she got most of the items on sale and she was only too happy to meet and entertain some of my shipmates.

We had just gotten a coastwise payoff and had signed on for a foreign voyage so I was not bad off financially. I sent some money to relatives back east and deposited the rest in the bank. I reminded Betty that I hadn't given her a Christmas gift yet. I splurged by giving Betty the gift of a free month's rent in her apartment. Her rent was only 95 dollars but I gave her a hundred and told her to keep the change. She had given me an expensive looking bath robe, something I never wear but was thankful for.

9

JAPAN

When I returned to the ship I was hoping to hear the sailing time had been delayed. Maybe we'd get an extra day in the Bay Area. It was just wishful thinking on my part. As I boarded, the sailing board read: "Ship sails 08:00 Tuesday January 24; Yokohama, Japan."

The twelfth and a half day crossing was not as rough as I expected especially judging from the route we took which was the Northern Circle Route. In late January, it was not exactly smooth sailing, but we didn't run into any typhoons or hurricanes on the way either. We had several fire and boat drills just in case. The ship's store opened several times to see that the crew was supplied with cigarettes, toiletries, and various other goodies. Those who indulged in alcoholic beverages managed to get their stash aboard without incident before leaving Oakland. The moderate drinkers had nothing to worry about. The ones who suffered with drinking problems surprisingly kept their problems swept under the rug. They covered their jobs without being a hazard to the ship or themselves and not giving Captain Schraeder a reason to make a raid on living quarters and working spaces. The average captain appreciated not having that worry.

About two nights before reaching Yokohama, K.O. called Charlie and me into his room. He broke out his stash of Irish whiskey. I went for a bowl of ice. Irish whiskey was never my drink of choice but I played along to be sociable and so did Charlie. Bruce, who was in his office doing paperwork, declined K.O.'s invitation, but Jesse was right there. He could care less about the brand of alcohol as long as he could quench his thirst. Bob Harris came in and had one drink for the road begging forgiveness for a long and mean day out on deck. That left the four of us there to talk about the trip ahead.

All of us had traveled to the Far East before but the others in the room had been there more recently. I hadn't been there since my Navy tour, 12 and a half years earlier. They laughed at me telling me how expensive Japan had become and how much more money I would be spending to have a really good time ashore. I told them that it was no big thing. We would only spend two nights in Yokohama and one of those nights would be spent renewing old acquaintances with a Navy couple I knew from Norfolk. Charlie spoke up saying he would look up a girlfriend he met nearly a year ago. He laughed saying if she wasn't still available, there were plenty more where she came from. Jesse said he would have a ball ashore come what may. Women yes, but the primary objective would be to get his head back on straight. I had noticed from the previous trip that when Jesse engaged in lengthy conversation about his wife while onboard, he indulged in excessive drinking the next time ashore. Both Charlie and I expressed concern about his behavior during this particular trip especially later on when we were in Vietnam.

We poured ourselves several more rounds of Irish whiskey then it was K.O.'s turn to have the floor. He sat on the corner of his bunk and leaned against the bulkhead. He told us about his fancy for Oriental women. When it came to marriage and family he would stay with his own race. But when playing around he preferred Oriental girls, especially the Chinese. He confessed that he was getting more and more involved with them since he began making these trips to the Far East and Southeast Asia. They really turned him on. He said they treated him so special, even better than his wife did back home. I took note that K.O. was a handsome young man much younger than the rest of us, still in his twenties. I thought at the time that he would get away from harboring such fantasies as he grew older. Then again, maybe he wouldn't. We fell silent while K.O. continued telling about his passion then Jesse butted in telling about his passion for mixed-race women from South Africa. He was so smitten by one of them he married her and brought her back to the States. Then Charlie spoke up. He could no longer hold his peace.

"I've been all over the world and slept with all races of women," he said, "but I always come back to my Black wife. Sometimes I call her Sapphire. We've been married over 45 years. I wouldn't trade her for all the women in the world. I'll stick with my Black woman until death do us part."

"Your prerogative," Jesse said just above a whisper.

K.O. didn't comment further. He knew that for the next several months, while we were in the Orient, he could and would have all the women of his choice. As for the rest of us during this time we would hold the attitude that a woman is a woman whatever her race might be. Without such an attitude we would more than likely end up doing without a girl, a choice that we weren't going to let happen.

As the night wore on we continued the conversation about different parts in the Far East and Southeast Asia. My three drinking partners had been to many or most of them. I had only been to three ports in Japan and two in the Philippines. With my limited knowledge of what the voyage would be like I did more listening than talking and asked a few questions along the way. These guys knew girls in almost every port. In most cases the girls would be there waiting when they hit the bars. If a girl was special enough, they would pen a note ahead letting them know they were on the way. In some of these ports we would stay two to five days; in others we might be lucky enough to get a week or more. It depended on how much cargo was to be offloaded or backloaded, the efficiency of the longshoremen, and whether there were any breakdowns. The stay was usually short in Yokohama as there was not much cargo. The stop was mainly to refuel.

It was nearly 23:00 before our visit with K.O. broke up. I would get to bed and still be up and about before our call out at 06:00 the next morning. I admit the four whiskeys on the rocks were catching up with me. K.O. had insisted that we serve ourselves with a heavy hand.

The next evening after dinner all of us in the Steward Department worked in the storerooms with Bruce for several hours. It was overtime pay and naturally we all jumped at the opportunity. K.O. and Ken worked in the freezer and chill boxes rearranging some meats, fruits, and vegetables. I preferred working in the dry stores where heavy jackets or sweaters were never needed. We all finished by 21:00.

Back in the Recreation Room, up walked Ken with a sly grin on his face. He called Charlie, K.O., Jesse, and me to his quarters. Juan politely declined. He knew it would be an invitation for alcohol. Juan never drank aboard ship. Being a retired sailor, I guess it was a carryover from his years in the Navy. He did all his drinking ashore. Ken on the other hand, drank only beer aboard ship. He drank whiskey ashore and wine with dinner when in the company of a lady, preferably his wife. We had the same taste in spite of his Tennessee background. We both enjoyed Kentucky bourbon straight. I only had two Budweisers with Ken because I knew the next day would be quite busy as we came into port. After clearing with the customs agents there would more than likely be some Japanese guests aboard for lunch. There would also be Japanese vendors in the passageways peddling their wares. We would be in by 10:00. The Deck and Engine Departments would be even busier. With all of that in mind we broke with the beer and opted for an early night.

◆　　◆　　◆

Coming into the harbor the next day Mt. Fuji looked very good. We were going to be at anchorage off Yokohama, not at the pier. Being at anchorage made offloading and going ashore a little inconvenient but it was better than being at sea. We would be going ashore in a launch to the South Pier, not too far from the center of the city. Charlie told me it would be alright with Bruce if I took off after lunch. He would cover dinner for me.

"Don't come back until tomorrow morning," he said.

After double checking with Bruce, I caught the 13:00 launch. I had written my friends Diane and Jerry, from Oakland. I planned to meet them at the Naval Enlisted Men's Club at 14:00 or at the Seamen's Club at 15:00. I was off until the next morning, but I would voluntarily return to the ship by midnight because, with the ship at anchorage, I felt safer that way.

◆　　◆　　◆

I took a taxi to the Seamen's Club after getting off the launch. I dropped off some mail and went straight to the bar where I met up with Diane and Jerry. I hadn't seen them in nearly five years. We shouted and hugged each other as the other customers looked on curiously. I told them about getting their address from a barmaid in Ocean View named Janie. She had told me about their transfers first to San Diego and then overseas to Yokohama.

Diane and Jerry were a young White couple I had met in Norfolk in the early 1960's. Those were the waning years of segregation there. Jerry and I were both in the Navy and Diane was a dutiful naval wife. Jerry was a very gifted Second Class Electrician. They had been shopping at the Navy Exchange. They lived in a fancy apartment building on Granby Street near the High School. I learned that Jerry, like me, was on a destroyer docked at the Submarine Piers. He was soon going to a ship in San Diego. I envied them getting away from Norfolk.

We met when they gave me a lift from the main base to a bus stop off Hampton Boulevard. It was cold and rainy that day. I had just managed to pick up a jug at the Open Mess. I was on my way to see some friends of mine, Dean and Joyce. I offered to pay them for the ride, but they refused any money.

As I got out of the car, Jerry gave me their address and telephone number. He told me I was welcome to attend a bon voyage party his friends and shipmates were throwing for them. That really delighted me. Diane and Jerry included me in their social affairs, not caring that I was a complete stranger or that I was Black.

The party was three weeks later. I was not comfortable going alone but my friends were mostly from Church Street bars and didn't fit in, or had any desire to pretend. Dean and Joyce came to my rescue like they always did. I would escort a friend of Joyce's who was a nurse at one of the local hospitals. Joyce and Dean would be most happy to go along with us. We attended the going away party in the suburb of Norview and a good time was had by all.

Here we were face to face again almost five years later. They were both in their early thirties. Their children, a ten year old daughter and six year old son, were back in the States with Diane's parents. Diane still looked attractive; slim and trim. Jerry on the other hand had gained a few pounds but still had his youthful face. He had risen to First Class Electrician shortly after leaving Norfolk and was now a Chief Electrician. I congratulated him on rising to the top of the enlisted men's ladder.

We had an enjoyable evening together beginning with a brief stop at their apartment and then on to a grand tour of the bars in Chinatown and on Izizaki Cho Street. We then went to a Military club. As a civilian, I was wondering how I would get in. Dianne and Jerry talked to the man at the door and I was whisked inside and introduced to some of their friends. It was a really nice place. We had drinks and dinner and spent the next four hours talking about Norfolk, San Diego and what had been happening in our lives over the last five years. I told them about some bars closing on both sides of town and the decline of Norfolk's Main and Church Streets. Jerry said it was good riddance. He thought the same about some sections of San Diego. I told them Janie sent her regards. Jerry thought she should get out of Ocean View, but couldn't say where she should go if she did escape.

I told them I had become a Merchant Mariner working on ships carrying both commercial and Military cargo around the world. Several of the other Chiefs at our table were about to retire. They wanted to know how easy it would be for them to ship out after retiring from the Navy. I told them it would be fairly easy. They wanted to know where I was traveling to after Yokohama. I apologetically explained that I couldn't go into details about the voyage for security reasons. They understood and so did their ladies.

Our group was holding their alcohol fairly well; Diane and Jerry always did. The club as a whole was very orderly with a sizable number of Military couples coming and going. As usual, when a good time is being had by all, the time seems to go by so much faster. It was already 22:15 when I thanked Jerry and Diane for a wonderful evening. I declined their offer to put me up for the night since I had to rise early the next morning. After handshakes and hugs, I promised to keep in touch and tore myself away from the party. It was a good reunion. By 23:00 I was on the South Pier catching a launch back to the *Marine Charger*. Ken and Bruce were already aboard.

◆　　◆　　◆

As we boarded the ship, I noticed there was no sailing information posted. Instead, the board was notifying the crew that we would be moving from anchorage off the South Pier to docking at the North Pier. This was good news because it meant that I could go ashore for some shopping between lunch and dinner the next day. Either South or Center Pier would have been more convenient, but beggars couldn't be choosy. I went on to bed knowing it would be another busy day tomorrow.

Getting through breakfast the next morning was a breeze. Charlie had everything in place from the storeroom and chill box. I set the tables and we were ready to serve. Some of the crew had spent the night with their girlfriends which meant less people to serve and less clean up afterwards. When I was done scrubbing the deck, I went to visit with Charlie. He told me he had run into a girl he knew from years past.

"Good for you," I told him.

I wanted to know if she knocked him out. He said it was the other way around in spite of almost 40 years difference in age. He went on about his work with unusual pep. K.O. and Jesse spent the night ashore. They too had found girls from their past.

◆　　◆　　◆

I made two long distance telephone calls early in the day; one to Betty and one to Adrian. The time differences were 17 and 15 hours earlier than Yokohama, respectively. My afternoon trip ashore was strictly to shop for gifts and souvenirs. We were getting about 360 yen to the dollar back then. I had a taxi take me to the silk center.

The silk center was a sight to behold! There were uncut bolts of silk of every color and pattern. Now would be the time to give my lady friends a well deserved treat. I purchased five yards of a beautiful gold silk for each of four ladies including Betty and Adrian. It would make lovely after-five cocktail dresses. I also found silk kimonos that I would later mail to Judy back in Sydney and to an old friend back east. I bought two smoking jackets for some old drinking buddies back in Denver. For myself, I picked up two large ashtrays for the coffee table.

◆   ◆   ◆

I returned to the ship to serve dinner and convinced Charlie, with so much of the crew ashore, I could cover dinner for both of us. That gave him another night out with his young girlfriend who was waiting for him at the bar.

◆   ◆   ◆

After a quick clean up, I was in a taxi on my way to Chinatown. I paid off the driver and turned to face a whole strip of bars. I went into one called *The Swallow* and was lucky enough to run into K.O. He had a lovely girlfriend at his side. K.O. made the introductions and asked me to have a drink with them. I never like to hinder social progress, but he insisted so I had one for the road. He said he had known his girl for nearly two years. Her name was Mishako. All through my brief visit with them she wore a shy smile on her face. K.O. certainly had good taste in women. It was about 19:30 when I bought them a round of drinks and left *The Swallow*. As I was leaving, I watched a large group of American servicemen being greeted at the door by an even larger group of Japanese hostesses.

As I wandered down the street, I passed *The Scandinavian*. I had heard about it onboard ship. They catered strictly to seafarers from northern European countries like Sweden and Norway. It, like all the bars, had an abundance of Japanese hostesses to take care of the sailor's needs and a dutiful Japanese bartender. As an African American, I would have been served, but chances are I would otherwise be ignored.

I had also been warned that some restaurants and clubs in Japan were for Japanese only. They wouldn't serve Americans no matter what their skin color was. At that point I realized that I had traveled to the other side of the world and could still see racism raise its ugly head.

I walked down the street and around the corner where I found *The Blue Canary*. I knew I had hit pay dirt. This was where quite a number of Soul brothers and sisters, both Military and civilian, met to kick back and have a good time. The bar was run by a Japanese woman who was once married to a Merchant Seaman. When they broke up he returned to the States. She stayed in Japan to run the bar. I went in to find the place almost filled to capacity. There were a few Japanese girls in there along with Soul sisters who were mostly Military dependants. The few White males there were servicemen and Merchant Seamen looking for action. There were a few couples on the dance floor and the waitresses were busy serving drinks. Mamasan, the owner, seemed to be sitting on a goldmine.

I spotted Jesse and Bob Harris through the crowd. Their girlfriends were sitting with them. Two extra girls were sitting at the next table. I asked one of them, Oyama, for a dance. When we returned to the table, Bob and Jesse were starting to get loud, especially Jesse. The girls were smiling as they sipped their watered down drinks. Bob, Jesse, and their lovely girlfriends soon headed for the door with the girls ordering my shipmates to walk steady. Any crew spending the night ashore would have to head back early since the ship was sailing early the next morning.

It was just before 21:00 and I decided to stay at *The Blue Canary* awhile longer. Some of the customers were very friendly and we introduced ourselves to each other. I took Oyama to the dance floor once more. Despite eating dinner on the ship, I was starting to get hungry. Oyama was a darling of a girl. She offered to fix me a bowl of noodles at her place. I jumped at the offer. We tarried for about another half an hour in which I returned a round of drinks to a Military dude and his girl sitting nearby.

◆　　◆　　◆

As we left, I waved to Mamasan who returned my greeting with a smile. It was unusually cold for February in Japan. When the night air hit me I sobered up on the spot. As we walked along the strip I was ready to get out of the cold. Oyama saw several people she knew among the customers entering and leaving the bars. Taxis were readily available and soon we were hopping into one. Minutes later we were at her door. It had been so long since I had visited Japan, I forgot that their customs required me to remove my shoes before entering her home. I remembered as she began removing hers. Her home was close quarters but I could feel an invisible welcome sign all over the place. She fixed the noodles for me. I was still shivering from the cold night air. Oyama handed me a cup and poured me some hot tea. As the noodles were cooking, they carried what seemed to be a fish aroma. Noodles and tea; what a combination! I paid her up front for treating me so royal. After I finished eating, Oyama rubbed my face and back until I was no longer cold. During the massage, she spoke to me switching back and forth from Japanese to English. I was puzzled, but fairly certain I was not returning to the ship that night.

"No cold," Oyama said as she rolled the bed out on the floor and put a heavy quilt on it.

I remembered my visits to Yokosuka, Sasebo, and Kobe nearly a decade ago. Japan had become a bit more expensive but one thing hadn't changed. The girls still knew how to give their male guests a darn good time. What a night!

Oyama woke me early the next morning in plenty of time to get back to the ship. I told her I was not ready to go yet.

"Please just a little while longer?" I asked as we kissed and played a friendly game of tug-of-war with the quilt.

Her shrewd instinct told her she had better get me out of there and in a taxi within the next half an hour or I would be in trouble big time. After a little more playing around, I got up and Oyama helped me get washed. She saw me to the taxi and we promised each other that we would keep in touch. A promise I kept for many years.

◆   ◆   ◆

I returned to the ship to learn that the sailing board now read: "Ship sails 08:00; Busan, South Korea." As I boarded I was greeted by a Japanese tailor running toward me with my new suit in his hands. He had measured me the day before for a gray silk mohair suit. Since the ship was sailing in a few hours, he wanted to close all the deals before we left port. I could hardly believe my eyes. I immediately rushed to my quarters and tried it on. I had no complaints whatsoever; it fit like a glove. This was the first suit I ever owned made of that material. Here I was wearing an amazing suit which cost me only 50 dollars. After I double thanked him, I paid him for the suit and gave him a five dollar tip. With a broad grin, he bowed his head slightly in an act of sincere gratitude.

I would go on with my work, making it through the day and waiting to make some after dinner comparisons with fellow crew members on our Japanese experiences. I thought of Japan as a port of no nonsense. If you don't start any trouble, there won't be any trouble. No street hustling or begging going on. They valued their privacy which is understandable. I gave Oyama a fairly good sum for her favors. I woke up with not a penny or a yen missing from my person. Regretfully, this was not the case in other ports of the Far East and Southeast Asia. I met good people but some of them were much less hospitable than those in Japan.

10

SOUTH KOREA

The short trip to Korea went without incident. We docked in the middle of everything. The center of activity was in walking distance if you had the energy. We were in an Army compound with South Korean Army personnel all around. You walked outside the gate, took a right turn, and in a short distance there you were at the Seamen's Club. This club was strictly civilian for Merchant Seamen but catered to anybody who walked in. There were American soldiers as customers as well as Korean girls, some without escorts. The place was lively. Since I didn't bother to have dinner before leaving the ship, I checked out the menu. As expected all the waitresses and cooks were Korean. I decided on a medium steak, baked potato with sour cream, and vegetables. Since I intended to do a little drinking I decided to skip dessert. The meal was filling enough anyway. My compliments went to the chef.

After dinner I headed to Texas Street where much of the action was. I went straight to *The Anchor* bar which I heard would be full of girls. Many of my fellow crewmen would be there also. A cold beer would do the trick to wash dinner down, then on to whiskey. My drinking buddies Bruce, Charlie, Jesse, and Bob were already there. Each had a girl at their side. Yes, K.O. and Ken were at a corner table each with a girl too. I jokingly told them they were in the middle of a dream. Ken laughed and said okay, but K.O. warned me not to try waking him up. A girl with a tray in her hand had just served some American sailors. I asked her to find me a seat. Right away she handed her tray to another girl and placed me in a seat at a table with two other girls. She then sat with me asking me what I wanted. I ordered a beer and she got it right away. I paid for it then she sat down again making me feel at home. She gave her name as Kim, a common name among Koreans both male and female. I told her to call me Buzz.

"Work out, Buzz," Jesse yelled across the bar.

He was so many sheets to the wind that I decided to ignore the comment and just return his greeting with a friendly wave. His girlfriend was doing a splendid job of adult babysitting. It seemed we were all really enjoying ourselves. Kim was a fairly nice looking girl. She looked a little younger than the age she gave me, which was 25. Two more girls joined us at the table. Each had a bowl of noodles. It made me think of Oyama back in Yokohama. One thing was different. Things were a bit cheaper in Busan. People in general were more independent minded in Japan. That would be noticed in all walks of life.

I had no desire to walk around that night. The weather was just as cold in Korea as it had been in Japan. I noticed that the girls in Busan were not restricted to the bars they worked in or frequented. They could go around town with their new-found boyfriends whether it was bar hopping or souvenir shopping. I asked Kim to have dinner with me at the Seamen's Club the next night. She jumped at the idea. We spent several more hours at *The Anchor* before she invited me to spend the night at her home.

"I thought you'd never ask," was my reply.

She lived not too far from the bar. It was nearly 11:00 PM. All of my drinking buddies had left with their girlfriends in tow but *The Anchor* was still in a party mood. There was really no hurry except that I wanted to get to a home atmosphere with a lady's touch.

◆   ◆   ◆

Kim's apartment was small, neatly arranged to the last object. We sat visiting for awhile. I assured her I was alright. She asked for a small amount of money. I was happy to oblige. I warmed up quickly from our walk in the night air. When we bedded down, I noticed and felt a large thick quilt. This time the bed wasn't rolled out on the floor, but rather a regular bed like you'd find anywhere in the States. Kim gave me such a goodnight at her place I almost forgot about our dinner date. When I was ready to leave we agreed to meet at *The Anchor* at 7:00 PM the next night. Taxis were cruising by almost like in New York. I did not have to call one. The friendly driver got me back to the ship in less than five minutes.

◆   ◆   ◆

My routine duties on the ship were quiet. At lunch I chatted briefly with Sully. As Chief Officer, he was quite busy overseeing the handling of cargo and many other activities onboard. As I served him a bowl of soup, I remarked that I hadn't seen him ashore in Yokohama or Busan. He came back with a sharp attack saying he had better things to do than throw his money away on those "whores."

He also said it would be alright to pick up some gifts but he didn't see anything he hadn't gotten for his wife years ago. I then decided to let well enough alone. I asked Martinjak, who was sitting at the Engineer's table, about his shore activities.

"Hell yes, I'm going ashore. I'm getting off this ship every chance I get."

"Same here," said Sheehan, the Second Mate, who was rushing through a quick lunch before going shopping.

He would have to return before 16:00 for his watch. For most of the crew, it was party time in Korea. Getting around was convenient and attractive girls to party with were easily available.

♦   ♦   ♦

Kim and I met up as planned at 7:00 PM. She was really dressed for the occasion, wearing a navy blue coat over a light colored dress, complete with black high heel shoes. I wore a gray suit, white shirt, and blue tie with black shoes of course. I added a black coat to protect myself from the cold night.

♦   ♦   ♦

At the Seamen's Club, Kim was looking around in awe at the many things available, especially on the menu. I told her to take her time ordering. She didn't have a good knowledge of reading an English menu, so one of the waitresses assisted her. She decided on a Korean dish of noodles and vegetables. I went the same route as the night before, a steak dinner with the works. We both decided on Cokes instead of alcoholic beverages.

The club was crowded. Some American sailors were there off a ship in the seventh fleet. Kim and I took our time finishing our dinner and making small conversation.

After dinner we drifted around the club playing a few games on the machines. We saw several crew members from the ship. I introduced her to them and their girlfriends. Kim and the other girls exchanged brief conversation in Korean. A short time later we were on our way back to *The Anchor*. There, it was party time all over again. We table hopped, getting acquainted with each other as we listened to the music. It seemed like nobody was a stranger. I was getting a buzz and enjoying it all. The girls were happy to see all of us having a good time. They mostly egged us on with applause and giggles. Time moved fast. It was about time to part company with the other guests.

We left my drinking buddies and their girlfriends in the bar. In spite of being older men with duties to perform early the next morning, they were not ready to call it a night just yet. More power to them.

Kim made a point to see that I didn't get cold in or out of her home. She dutifully fastened the top button on my coat as we walked out of the bar. We got inside her place after waving goodnight to the taxi driver. The smirk on his face told me he knew just what was happening.

◆   ◆   ◆

Once inside, Kim took off my coat and shoes going out of her way to make me feel at home. She then handed me a non-alcoholic drink. I handed her a 20 dollar bill telling her to keep the change. She hugged me and kissed me on both cheeks. Before long we were undressed and off to bed for another enjoyable night.

The next morning before walking out of the door, we had a serious chat. Kim knew I would soon be leaving Busan. It would be a long time before I returned, if ever. She understood, but I was beginning to develop an attached feeling as well as a lump in my throat. Unlike most of my shipmates I found it difficult to have a good time with these women and then forget them after the ship sails. I would not get as serious as K.O. and Jesse, but it was becoming harder and harder to say goodbye. It would have been different if all these women had been hustlers or streetwalkers, but some of the girls I had relations with recently, never asked for money. In the States and in Australia, women wined and dined me and any monetary gifts I gave were strictly voluntary. In Yokohama and Busan it was strictly a business deal with money up front. But I still got the royal treatment for very little cash.

I had taken a job that would put the entire Pacific Ocean, the Gulf of Mexico, and now the South China Sea between me and my loved ones. And it was easy to become attached to these beautiful women. Kim insisted I not forget her on my next trip to Busan.

"Definitely not," was my reply.

After some more hugs and kisses, I got in the taxi and was on my way back to the ship.

11

WAR ZONE—PART 1

The sailing board read: "Da Nang, Vietnam." An eerie feeling came over me. It was hard to believe that in about a week's time I would be smack in the middle of a War Zone.

It was a bit choppy at sea the first several days and the weather was still a bit on the chilly side. The further south we sailed, the warmer the weather got. Soon we would be in the tropics, which would be alright by me.

While sailing between San Francisco and Yokohama we had held a Union meeting to bring the crew up to date and brief newcomers on the rules and regulations expected by the head office in New York. Now another meeting was called to stress safety regulations and detail how we were to conduct ourselves in the War Zone. Whether it was about the different colors of alert or possible terrorist approaches by the Viet Cong, I listened carefully to what they had to say.

Sully spoke of the nightly curfews. We would have to be off the streets by 23:00. The American Military wielded all of the authority here. It would be unwise to give them any trouble. I had no intentions of giving anybody any trouble, but one thing for sure I intended to spend very little time off the ship while we were in the War Zone.

◆　　◆　　◆

The night before coming into port all the gang in the Steward's Department got together in the Recreation Room, except Larry the Bedroom Steward. After working hours he usually kept to himself. We started talking about Vietnam as a whole. I was all ears since it was my first trip there. K.O. and Jesse took the floor first. Bruce would cut in occasionally when he thought they needed to be corrected. Bruce had been there more times than anybody on the ship.

"Don't violate curfew!" was his advice. "Whether you're with a woman or coming back to the ship, get there before curfew begins."

Charlie, Jesse, and K.O. said they would be with their women come what may. Dale and Jake were all ready for adventure. They were listening to the wisdom of much older seafarers. Later they would have a mind of their own.

Both Ken and Juan said they were going to be on deck before the ABs dropped the gangway. The only way they were staying aboard is if they got restricted. The beer and whiskey started flowing. That particular night all of the crew was well behaved. Everybody was excited about coming into Vietnam. Bob tried to tell them it was going to be just another port, of course hardly any of us believed him. I for one would be seeing for myself and playing it by ear. I just kept sipping my Budweiser and thinking about how far I had come in less than three months. I was still a distance away from journey's end.

It was now just before midnight. All of us in the Steward Department began drifting off to bed and so did those in the Deck and Engine Departments who were not on watch.

◆   ◆   ◆

The next morning at 08:00 we were docking in the harbor off Da Nang. I was able to watch the docking from the deck since I had finished serving breakfast early. The picturesque harbor was a sight to behold as it sat at the foot of a green mountain.

"Vietnam, here I am," I said to myself.

A non-stop line of Military vehicles made their way slowly around a winding road en route between the Navy Station and the ships in the harbor. They passed nonchalantly through a checkpoint. I heard some of the cargo was also going to Phu Bai, the Marine Base across the river.

Just about all of the longshoremen were U.S. Navy personnel. They were dressed in Army green fatigues and hard hats instead of the traditional dungarees, blue shirts, and work caps. They were very efficient in their work. Heavy traffic continued all through the day both on the pier and aboard ship.

Some of us from the ship decided to stretch our legs after lunch by going out on deck. We would eventually hitch a ride to the base to see whether we would be allowed to use the Post Office and Navy Exchange. No such luck. A young Navy guard at the checkpoint stopped the four of us from going any farther. He told us that in the past we were allowed base privileges, but no more. He apologized but said he was under orders not to allow any civilians to go past his checkpoint. We were disappointed but realized the guard was doing nothing more than covering his job. We had no choice but to return to the ship.

The sailors kept working on the cargo coming into the Crew Mess for short coffee breaks. We learned from them that the town was not off limits since there was no alert. There was a launch going across the bay from the dock. Most of the off duty crew jumped at the idea of going ashore. But a few, myself included, decided to first get up a little more nerve before spending the night ashore in Vietnam. K.O., as expected, was one of the first crew members on the launch. Charlie and Jesse weren't far behind. They were the only three in our department to take advantage of the situation. Almost all off duty persons in the other departments went ashore. I chilled two beers and called it a night.

◆   ◆   ◆

The next day there were two extra people to serve in the Saloon Mess: a Lieutenant J.G. and a Chief Petty Officer. They were in some way associated with the movement of the cargo. They got carried away with the many menu choices, something the crew took for granted. I would not have been surprised if it had been their first time being served on a non-Military ship.

"What a meal," the Chief said of their lunch.

The second night in port I realized I was getting low on beer. Being a moderate drinker, I was going slowly on alcohol. Whiskey was no sweat. I had stocked up on bourbon and rum before leaving the States. But as the temperatures would be rising to more than one hundred degrees, I would be leaning more and more on beer to quench my thirst. That's where Martinjak came in. He was a good contact. Although he worked in the engine room as a First Engineer, he had a knack for meeting just the right longshoremen. Martinjak steered this contact to me. He told me to call him "Boats." I told him of my problem and he said he'd see what he could do. There was so much traffic on deck I would have to wait until after dark. Just before midnight, Boats knocked on my door.

"Open up!" he yelled.

He had a case of beer. He told me to take it and keep things under my hat. He had my word. I tried to pay him but he would not hear a word of it.

"Keep it," he ordered with a strong mid-Western accent.

"Thanks again," I replied.

I rushed to the ice machine and got a bucket of ice. I gave it to Boats to carry back on deck for him and his subordinates. I placed my liquid treasure under lock and key and went back to bed. I knew our third day in Da Nang would be getting warmer.

When I got up the next morning, I found the bucket at my door. While serving breakfast, the first thing I did was thank Martinjak for sending Boats my way. "Anytime," he said.

We talked in low tones out of earshot of his fellow officers. He left, strolling casually toward the Engine Room.

I took a special liking to Martinjak and Sully. The other officers were okay, but my dealings with them were always more formal. Martinjak would sometimes party with us when we were ashore. Aboard ship he would occasionally come down and drink with non-licensed personnel. He could really hang one on. Charlie was worried that it might be affecting his job performance, but he had managed to maintain it so far. Martinjak's mingling with the crew down below was fast becoming a "No-No" especially with the Captain and the Chief Engineer. Sully on the other hand, stayed on top and in control of his job. He would hang one on once in a while, but in spite of his advanced age he always managed to hold his own among the younger officers onboard.

◆　　　◆　　　◆

I went ashore after lunch, making the rounds of the bars and other establishments. It was obvious I was not in Japan or Korea. I declined Charlie's offer to cover dinner for me and was back to the ship in time to fulfill my duties. Bruce stayed aboard but Jesse, Charlie, and K.O. were off like rockets. They were eager to get ashore to meet up with their young girlfriends. Ken stayed aboard, but Bob decided at the last minute to go along. Old as he was, Charlie was the leader of the pack. They boarded the launch giggling like a bunch of middle school kids going out on their first date. Some of the sailors standing by looked on in disbelief.

The sailors and longshoremen worked the cargo with such speed and efficiency, all of us knew we would not be getting a week in Da Nang. On the fifth day, the sailing board was posted. We would be sailing at 20:00 to the harbor of Qui Nhon.

I spotted Boats leaving the ship and ran to catch up with him for a farewell handshake. He was busy with some of his workers. They were securing some gear adrift on the pier. In a little while the *Marine Charger* was cruising in the South China Sea. I knew the vision of the new piers, heavy traffic, and that tall green mountain in the background, would always be etched in my memory.

◆   ◆   ◆

Once in Qui Nhon, the name of the game was the same. The Military ran the show in the War Zone. This time the Army called the shots.

Like in Da Nang, I didn't venture ashore the first two nights. The majority of my drinking buddies did. They went on the prowl through the village and from what they said, they enjoyed themselves. After they waded through a crowd of begging kids and some hustling adult males, they found some Vietnamese women ready to give them a night of partying.

We spent almost a week in Qui Nhon offloading cargo. Then we all found out how unpredictable government contracts can be. After the ship was unloaded the Captain received orders to make a brief shuttle run to Kaohsiung ("Kow-Shung"), a port city in Taiwan. What the crew wasn't prepared for was that the ship would be loaded with ammunition and brought back to Vietnam. It would be a ten percent bonus pay for the ammunition being aboard.

Loading ammunition was a long drawn-out process so we were in Kaosiung almost ten days. It was an enjoyable time for most of us. The people were rather friendly. Sometimes it could be a task getting around the hustlers and beggars. Oh yes, there were girls galore. Most of us found a short cut around the riff-raff.

We would pick up our girlfriends at the bars and take them to the Military club for dining and dancing. There were a number of bars in downtown Kaosiung, but they could be expensive. They hustled as many drinks as they could make money for the bar as well as a percentage for themselves. With the Military club open to us, we took the girls there where it was much cheaper. If the price was right the girls would eventually take you home. My lady friend was nice, but very business like. I stuck with her the whole time we stayed in port. I called it an as-is deal. I had no desire to butterfly, going from one girl to another. She said her name was Li Un. I called her Li ("Lee"). I made sure I didn't get attached to her. It was strictly business and there were no sad songs on sailing day.

During our stay in Taiwan, we helped Bruce take on some stores including some fruits and vegetables. Most of the longshoremen were young Taiwanese men. There were some American Army supervisors. At first I felt uneasy about them handling the ammunition, as they seemed to be working so nonchalantly. As time wore on I came to realize that they wouldn't have been hired if they didn't know what they were doing.

The night before sailing all of us had a big party at the Military club. Some of the crew really went heavy duty buying such bamboo items as chairs and coffee tables to be shipped home later. Such items were not expensive at all. Sully bought a chair. He also had a young girl on his arm. He said she helped him pick out the chair as if he owed me an explanation.

All I could say was, "On with the show."

Whiskey and beer at a cheap price was flowing like water. Bruce, Charlie, Jesse, Bob, Ken, and Juan all had girls. Martinjak was walking around the club looking like an oversized lumberjack and feeling no pain. Most of the crew from the Deck and Engine Departments were maintaining. Some, like Martinjak, had the help of their girlfriends. There were also a few unescorted American women at the club. I guess they were dependants.

"We're having a good time and nobody is rocking the boat," I told my girl, Li.

We knew we had better enjoy our last party here, our female company too, so we stayed ashore another night. Coming back to the ship in the early morning hours, we were hungover but nevertheless ready to set sail for Cam Ranh Bay, Vietnam.

Once in a while a small fishing boat would come so close to the ship that the guard would fire a warning shot over their heads. I doubt these men were Viet Cong. Probably just lower income people trying to eke out a living in their troubled land.

◆   ◆   ◆

We would be a week in Cam Ranh Bay. It seemed that the monsoon rains were not over yet. In spite of the rain, the Army longshoremen and their Vietnamese assistants dove right in on the cargo. They unloaded the ammunition using extreme caution at all times and kept on schedule. I'm not sure about what was being backloaded, but something else was on the ship other than ammunition. Some of the soldiers were quite young, barely out of their teens, but showed skill and efficiency in the performance of their duties. There was an older Sergeant, who was Black, barking orders to his subordinates; keeping the peace as well as keeping them all in line. There was also a young, easy-going White Lieutenant who I served at lunch time. He looked more like someone in their senior year at West Point. It was his job to keep the records all straight.

Moreover he had a Sergeant he could depend on to keep the cargo moving in an orderly fashion. I observed how well they got along when they were in consultation. I found it to be quite commendable since Sgt. Franklin was from Delaware and Lt. Schley was from Mississippi. Lt. Schley would be leaving the Army after his tour in Vietnam was over while Sgt. Franklin had found a home in the

Military. In spite of a wife and family back in the States, he had been in the Army almost ten years and would be in the Army many more years to come.

◆   ◆   ◆

The second night in port I decided to go ashore, but not to the village. I just didn't trust going out there with alerts going off and on. There was a Seamen's Club just down the road in walking distance from the landing. There, nice meals were served and alcoholic beverages flowed. In such a setting you would think the party would be on. For a while I thought that way too. My thoughts were to be short-lived. At that time ships were coming to Cam Ranh Bay from U.S. ports far and near laden with cargo from the East, West, and Gulf Coasts. The Seamen's Club was the meeting place for civilian seafarers from all of these ships. Sometimes a few Army dudes would drift in and out. Often the Army would supply a small band for entertainment. Things should have gone quite orderly but they didn't. Some of the roughnecks brought on trouble by fighting with each other. They were carrying out grudges that began onboard their ships.

The Seamen's Club had a house rule that stated that the bar would be closed anytime a fight started and would remain closed until things were settled which sometimes took 20 minutes or more. Sometimes just as soon as one fight was over, another one started. I kept two drinks in front of me at all times in case there was a real knock down and drag out. Not all fights could be blamed on the guys on ships out of the gulf ports. Although they started their share, seafarers from the East and West Coasts were equally guilty. I saw this unbecoming conduct as a result of a lack of female companionship at the club. Very few women were around, except for employees, so the Seamen in many cases vented their frustrations by fighting each other. Several nights of witnessing such activity was enough to make me stay aboard a few nights. I would show back up at the club the last two nights before sailing. By that time, the riotous guys were many nautical miles out at sea and the club was in a peaceful setting.

◆   ◆   ◆

The next evening, after serving dinner, I put some beer on ice and decided to stay aboard. Charlie and Jesse also stayed aboard and surprisingly, Dale and Jake did too. I iced up three six packs. We all sat around in the room I shared with Charlie and talked about ports visited and ports to be visited. Jesse had brought a tall glass of scotch on the rocks from his room. He took one of my beers for a chaser and began to immediately take the floor. In walked the Chief Steward, Bruce, who opened a beer. Charlie was mellow and so were Dale and Jake. Our small room was full. Jesse started in on politics. I was in no mood to discuss politics. He started to talk about the "begging ass Vietnamese and Taiwanese." He wondered why they couldn't be more like the people in Japan and Korea where he could walk the streets and be left alone. You'd never be bothered in Japan by hustlers and beggars. Since nobody else was speaking up I decided to put my own two cents worth in. I told him the Vietnamese have not been industrialized for many centuries like the Japanese have been. The Vietnamese lived for many years under the yoke of colonialism and occupation by foreign powers including the French and the Japanese. Bruce interrupted by saying how he admired Japan for bouncing back so quickly after World War II. I told him they were able to utilize the aide offered by the United States. Due to their high degree of cultural and educational know how, they put to use the technology they had acquired from centuries past. I told them all that that was my own opinion, not necessarily the opinion of all others.

"You have a point," Jesse said as he took a sip of scotch.

"Thank you," I said. "Enough history lessons and politics for tonight."

The conversation switched to women in the Orient. Dale and Jake both thought these women could teach the American women a thing or two on how to treat their men. Charlie corrected him by telling him he was having a damn good time overseas, but as far as women went, he would always be looking forward to getting back to the woman he left behind. He was perfectly satisfied with the way she was treating him.

The conversation continued on with talk of wine, women, and song until after the usual 23:00 countdown. When everybody had drifted to their own rooms, I stepped out on deck. I saw the cargo handling still going full swing. When I returned to the room Charlie was already asleep. I looked in the bucket and saw that I still had two beers left for another occasion. I called it a night.

The fourth day in Cam Ranh Bay, I ran into a slick Puerto Rican soldier named Ramon Rodriguez. He was one of the cargo handlers. We hit it off very well. He was straight out of the South Bronx and only 21 years old, but he had the wisdom and knowledge of many 40 year olds I have known. I gave him lunch from the Crew Mess, which included a Reuben sandwich and some soup. I had no trouble getting a return favor since he preferred our menu to the rations the Army was offering. Ramon, Ray for short, sent one of his co-workers, Fred Miller, to give me some beer and a jug of Bacardi that night. Fred was a Soul brother, just as slick as Ray. He knew how to maneuver around his fellow workers who happen to be senior in rating or rank. I almost jumped out of my shoes when he told me he was from Kentucky. I told him I attended college many years earlier in Frankfort. He was from Covington, just across the river from Cincinnati. I was happy Fred didn't get caught. I could hardly thank him enough. I went up topside and gave the rum to Martinjak who, after thanking me, immediately started making Cuba Libres. Fred had to get on duty. He was very happy with the tip I gave him. Alcohol was dirt cheap there, being tax free.

◆   ◆   ◆

All of us in the Steward Department had been worried about Jesse. We were concerned about his excessive drinking and that he would one day explode. He did just that on Saturday afternoon in the middle of working dinner. He put on a real performance. His starring role started in the early afternoon. He had been drinking all morning. Right after lunch he went out on deck and started engaging in conversation with the soldiers on duty. Sgt. Franklin interfered, telling Jesse he was interrupting progress and asked him to leave his men alone.

"Carry your Black ass!" Jesse told the Sarge. "These soldiers are working hard and deserve the right to speak with me for a few seconds if they want to."

"Shove off!" shouted the Sarge.

"You can't order me. I'm a civilian," Jesse shouted back.

Sgt. Franklin was ready to tear Jesse to pieces. I ran back inside and got Bruce who was in his office. Bruce came out and ordered Jesse back inside. He was staggering along ahead of Bruce as they headed inside. Sarge was really furious. Jesse had made him look small in front of his workers. The two Black soldiers, who had been talking with Jesse, had embarrassed looks on their faces. The other soldiers looked puzzled; a few had smirks on their faces. Bruce came back and apologized to the Sarge. Sgt. Franklin got his men back to work. Lucky for Jesse, Sgt. Franklin didn't make mince meat out of him. Bruce and I agreed that the time and place wasn't right. Sarge had too much to lose.

Jesse was not through yet. After our two hour break between lunch and dinner, he went into the Galley trying to stagger through his duties. It was not to happen. About half way through, one of the guys complained to his watch partner that there was too much gel in the pie at lunchtime. Then one of the Crew Messmen brought Jesse a message from the Radio Officer that he didn't get enough beans on his order of chili beans and rice. I took his bowl back to the Galley and asked Jesse to add some more beans without telling him what the Radio Officer had said. That was the last straw.

Jesse dropped everything and walked into the Crew Mess cursing. He berated anybody in the crew who had the nerve to criticize his cooking. He suggested that anybody who wasn't satisfied with his cooking could go and get that woman they make their allotment to do their cooking.

"Kiss my Black ass!" Jesse shouted as he stumbled out of the Crew Mess. He went into the Saloon Mess and repeated the same words to the officers. They were stunned, especially Captain Schraeder and Sully. Both Mess Halls fell into silence. The Galley crew said nothing. K.O. just shook his head.

"Get the hell out!" shouted Bruce when Jesse tried to come back into the Galley to resume taking dinner orders.

◆   ◆   ◆

Charlie muttered what a damn shame it was. In his drunken and uncontrolled behavior Jesse had shown his true mannerisms. Bruce took over his duties until the end of dinner. Jesse made it to his room and passed out. The Captain and Sheehan, who were on duty at the time, were in hot pursuit. They searched his room and found a full jug and an open jug of White Label scotch which they confiscated. When the Captain called Jesse to his office the next morning, he explained the charges brought against him. They were mainly being drunk on duty and having alcohol onboard ship. Sully was present as well as Juan, the Steward Department's delegate. Bruce spoke up for Jesse telling the Captain he was one of his best workers when sober, but just couldn't handle his drinking. The Captain listened, but was bound by Guard regulations to cover his job.

Jesse was told his name would be entered in the log book for these offenses and he would be dismissed from the vessel at the end of the voyage. Jesse acted humble as he admitted to the charges brought against him, but made no apology for his disrespectful behavior. He returned to work in the Galley hardly engaging in any conversation with the crew except in the line of duty. Bruce and Charlie called me aside to offer some helpful advice. They told me not to give any more alcohol to Jesse. They said the Captain had two more crew members and an officer under surveillance for alcoholism. Their excessive drinking had begun to interfere with their ability to properly perform their duties. If push came to shove, the Captain would pull a raid on all living quarters as well as other parts of the ship and confiscate any alcohol found therein. Most captains looked the other way when their crew and officers drank onboard as long as they did it in a moderate way. When drinking onboard or ashore interfered with their work, these ships' captains had no choice but to crack down and crack down hard. After all, the Captain would be responsible for any injuries that occurred while a crew member or officer was in an intoxicated state of mind. No other way around it.

My Army friends, Fred and Ray, brought in some more beer the next day. Ray brought in two six packs. He was a real slickeroo, playing peek-a-boo to make sure no one else was around. I immediately stashed the beer in my locker. With K.O.'s permission, I came back and fixed Ray a fried chicken dinner and a glass of punch. He spoke a few phrases in Spanish then back to English thanking me.

"El gusto es mio," I answered, exercising my limited knowledge of Spanish, or "The pleasure is mine."

Most of the crew had already finished eating their lunch, so Ray decided to take his to the Crew Recreation Room.

"I'll return the dishes in a little while," he said with a grin.

Dale and Jake were just finishing up their lunches in the Crew Mess. I had finished serving in the Saloon Mess and Charlie was cleaning up the pantry when Ray came back with the empty dishes. As I put them in the sink to wash later, I had an idea. I asked Ray if he could bring Sarge to the Galley door. Maybe I should have let sleeping dogs lie, but I was determined to make the peace. Ray was back with Sgt. Franklin in what seemed like less than a minute. I called Jesse out of his room, bringing him face to face with Sarge. I told Jesse what he had said to Sarge the day before.

"Man, I was torn up," Jesse shamefully acknowledged.

"Forget it."

"I'm real sorry," Jesse said as he extended a trembling handshake to Sarge. "Is there anything I can get for you?"

"I'd like a piece of that chicken I smelled cooking."

K.O. had already left the Galley, but Jesse knew where he kept the leftovers. He got a chicken breast and a slice of apple pie, wrapped them in foil and handed them to Sarge.

"Thank you, man," Sarge told him. "You guys eat like kings."

Jesse also handed Ray a leg of chicken. Ray grabbed it like it was a prize of gold in spite of having just finished the lunch I gave him. Their noon break would be over in ten minutes. I told Ray I would see him the next day. Jesse told Sarge to come back to the Galley if he ever needed anything. Sarge thanked him again as he and Ray went back out on deck eating their fried chicken.

After they left, Jesse laughed and patted me on the back. He called me a peacemaker and jokingly wanted to know when I was going to join the United Nations. He stopped laughing quite suddenly.

"Thank you, Buzz."

I gave an affirmative nod, too overcome with relief to answer.

◆   ◆   ◆

After dinner on Sunday some of the crew went ashore to the village. Others, me included, went to the Seamen's Club. It was a far cry from a few nights before. I didn't have to keep two drinks in front of me tonight. The ships with the riotous crews had sailed to other ports. The band, a three piece combo made up of young Army dudes, provided fairly good entertainment. They were giving it their best shot playing and singing a few hit songs of the day. Surprisingly, there were no arguments or fights all night. I enjoyed getting out and stretching my legs, but I was back onboard ship long before the 23:00 curfew.

◆   ◆   ◆

I went to my room to get the two sirloin steaks I had put away for Fred Miller. I also had some French fries wrapped up with the steaks. I sat in the Recreation Room and waited for him to show up. I didn't have to wait long. Fred showed up with beer in a back pack. One of his White co-workers had come along. He introduced himself as Ron and reached out to shake hands with me. I read the name Ronald on his lapel and decided that it all jived out.

"Ron is from Kentucky too," Fred told me. "A town named Mayfield."

"I've heard of it," I told them. "Call me Buzz."

They both walked with me to my room. Bruce and Charlie were still sitting up on deck trying to catch a sea breeze and Jesse was in his bunk asleep. I was careful not to wake him, especially with beer in my possession. I quickly took the beer out of Fred's backpack and stored it in my locker. Fred refused the tip I offered, but gladly took the steak and fries. I also gave him a slice of pie leftover from lunch. He shared the meal with his friend, Ron. I walked with them back up on deck.

"Thanks, man," they said with their mouths full.

"Goodnight," I answered as they returned to work in the cargo hold.

The crew on the night shift seemed to be a little bit more relaxed than the day workers.

♦   ♦   ♦

On Blue Monday I had a short, chat with Lt. Schley while serving him his breakfast. Later he and Sarge met in the crew Recreation Room to discuss cargo handling. It was continuing on in a smooth fashion, which meant we would be sailing soon from Cam Ranh Bay.

I went ashore at 14:00 to visit the medical facility. I wanted to see for myself how the wounded were being cared for. There were soldiers there from the field and some local Military with minor ailments. I nodded hello to the personnel on bed rest. Those who seemed to be more seriously ill, I maintained my distance. The nurse, a young officer who obviously knew her way around, was very friendly. She said some of the patients would be fit to return to duty shortly while others would be transferred to other facilities to get the special treatment they needed. I wished the patients that I passed by on my way out a speedy recovery. It was time I got back to the ship to serve dinner. I thanked the nurse and medic for showing me around and left.

As I returned to the dock I wondered; if more young Americans could see what these young Military men and women in Vietnam were sacrificing, would they develop a different attitude about the war as a whole?

♦   ♦   ♦

That night after dinner Charlie, Jesse, Ken, and I sat out on the aft deck, out of the way of the men handling the cargo. We were all staying aboard tonight. A breeze was coming off the starboard that felt very good. I had iced a six pack of beer and four Cokes. Jesse and Charlie both grabbed Cokes. Ken and I took beer. We had a nice quiet evening. Some of the guys in the Deck and Engine Departments joined us later, bringing their own refreshments along. They talked about their experiences from years past including ports like Barcelona, Lisbon, Rio, and Santos. Some had had some beautiful memories to tell while others told sad, sad songs. I listened to all of them, forming my own opinions of what could have been or should have been. I could see that some of these men came out of retirement to pick up the pieces of their lives that just were not there anymore. Jesse remained quiet through all the sea stories and so did Ken. They had both already been through what these guys were talking about. Especially when discussing wine, women, and song. Before long, it was time to say another goodnight. I had three beers and two Cokes left in the bucket. As I walked to the room, I spotted

Fred and his work partner. I handed them the two ice cold Cokes from the bucket. They thanked me and chatted briefly before I continued on to my quarters. Charlie was already in bed when I got there.

The next morning I got up the nerve to ask K.O. for a favor. It was just after 09:00 when he was stirring pots and checking meats in ovens. I wanted him to fix me something that wasn't on the menu: a large beef, bean, and cheese burrito. Maybe he could fix it from some of the leftovers in the chill box. I could never pull the wool over his eyes. With his shrewd instinct and that sly smile on his face, I could tell that he knew this particular burrito was not for me to eat. I confessed that it was for a friend, one of the soldiers who had twice brought me beer "on-the-house."

"I appreciate the gifts every time I quench my thirst in this intense heat," I told K.O.

"Could it be done in time for lunch?" I asked. I assured him I would not make a habit of asking such special favors.

"You got it," he said.

He fixed a big burrito and handed it to me at lunch but said he expected two beers from me the first night at sea.

"It's a deal!" I said.

After thanking him, I went up to serve lunch. Charlie wrapped the burrito and kept it in the pantry for me.

Captain Schraeder came into the Mess and ordered a bowl of soup and a sandwich. The Chief Engineer, Grassi, was already seated eating his soup. All through lunch the Captain discussed the cargo operations with Grassi and made plans for the next port of call. The Radio Officer and the Purser strolled in and seemed to follow the Captain's lead, ordering soup and sandwiches. Due to the intense heat in Vietnam, many times going over one hundred degrees, much of the crew were sticking to light diets.

Ray came out of nowhere peeking into the Saloon Mess. Before the Captain or other officers could see him, I rushed outside and motioned to Charlie for the burrito. I poured him some Kool-Aid in a paper cup as he started biting into the burrito. He thanked me but I couldn't chat. I had to get back to work. I told Ray I would see him out on deck in about 20 minutes.

While we were talking on deck away from the hustle and bustle, along came Lt. Schley and Sarge. They were both in good moods. Lt. Schley, in his Southern drawl, thanked me for serving him such a good lunch. Sarge had eaten in the Crew Mess with the men. They walked on toward the cargo hold. As soon as they were out of earshot, Ray told me he would get me some more beer for the road.

"You don't have to," I said, "I'm okay."

He was taking a big risk, but he insisted. After all it was tax free. He continued eating the burrito saying how much he enjoyed it.

"The cook must have been Mexican," Ray stated.

"No," I said. "Irish eyes were smiling on that burrito."

I went on to tell him about Kevin O'Keefe's Culinary Arts degree and that, as Chief Cook, he could fix just about anything.

Ray's break was just about over and he returned to work. I went back inside for a nap before I had to serve dinner.

◆   ◆   ◆

The sailing board was set later that afternoon. We would be anchoring at the mouth of the Mekong River in a place called Vung Tau. We would wait there several days before transiting the river to Saigon.

The crew was very relieved to finally learn what direction we were heading. They flocked ashore for a last call in Cam Ranh Bay; a few went to the Seamen's Club, but most headed for the village. Whichever direction they went, it was party time. I went to the Seamen's Club for a couple rounds of drinks and listened to the band. I stayed through two intermissions then headed back to the ship. I got in touch with Fred and Ron one last time and gave them a couple of pork chop sandwiches saved from dinner. This meeting would be the last, at least for this trip. We thanked each other for favors and hospitality offered and I was on my way to bed. A few of the crew were still ashore looking for one more merry go around with a girl. More power to them.

Just after I finished serving the officers' breakfasts, I had my own. Jesse fixed me a big cheese omelet and some bacon. As I went into the Crew Mess to put on some toast, Jesse told me he wanted to talk to me. I was afraid he wanted some alcohol. He told me it was not about that, but since we'd all be aboard for sailing he'd like to talk to me about his wife and his trips to South Africa. Many of the crew and officers were still giving him the silent treatment because of his Saturday afternoon live episode. I was happy to see that a few were coming around to forgive and forget. Jesse was in a friendly mood and I told him I would be all ears right after dinner.

At lunch there was a run on the soup and sandwiches. The ham and cheese was quite tempting. A few took on the peach pie for dessert. Jesse had done such a superb job I couldn't resist having two helpings. When Ray showed up I told him to meet me at my quarters in 20 minutes. Martinjak was just walking out of the Saloon Mess. He nodded as if he knew just what was going on.

I had been in the room about five minutes when Ray knocked on the door. He took the six beers from the pack. I repeated my "thank you" then handed him the ham and cheese sandwich and a slice of the peach pie. Both were still warm and wrapped together. I told him to pick up a cold Coke out of the bucket near the door. He sat down and ate the lunch then drank his Coke. In his short break time, we talked about so much. He talked briefly about New York especially the South Bronx. He said he would love to get an R&R flight to Sydney.

"Girls and more girls," he told me.

"Been there!" I said.

"Sorry I have to rush off," Ray said as he headed back to the cargo hold.

They were just about finished loading the cargo. He gave me his home address to write him a card from some of the many places I would be traveling to around the world. After a firm handshake, I told him that I would write and he was out the door. I went to bed for my usual afternoon nap.

After rising about 15:30 I went in search of Lt. Schley and Sarge. I wanted to say so long. I found them out on deck near the gangway. I didn't stay long. I could see they both seemed quite occupied supervising the finishing touches. They told me our ship was the best as far as feeding guests and that they wanted us to hurry back.

"Many thanks," was my reply.

I gave a handshake to both of them and was on my way to the Saloon Mess to serve dinner.

After dinner I went out on deck for a brief spell. As the ship slowly sailed out of Cam Ranh Harbor I thought of the people I was leaving behind. We had just known each other a week, yet the friendship they extended to me made it seem like we had known each other for a number of years. Cam Ranh Bay as a whole would be a lifetime of memories.

I went back inside to check on Jesse. He invited me to his room for a chit chat. Bruce and Charlie were in the Recreation Room. K.O. was in his room reading and sipping a beer. The rest of the Steward Department were scattered somewhere around the ship. Just about everybody was excited about Vung Tau, those who had been there and those who hadn't. I had developed a wait and see attitude about this next port.

12

JESSE & JUHL

As I sat down in Jesse's room I couldn't believe what I saw. He had at least five beers iced in a bucket. He told me not to get excited. I reminded him of the trouble he was in already. He said Martinjak had sported him the beer providing he didn't rock the boat. He promised he wouldn't, at least no more. I opened a beer and slowly took a sip. Trying to change the subject right away we started talking about Jesse's many trips to South Africa.

Jesse was in his late thirties. He had been divorced by his wife ten years earlier in Louisiana. He had two children, first a girl and then a boy two years later. After the divorce he started taking shipping jobs from New Orleans to Cape Town, South Africa.

In Cape Town, Jesse met a fair skinned, mixed-race girl named Juhlene DeGroot. They hit it off right away. Whether it was love at first sight remained to be seen. He called her his Juhl ("Jewel"). Jesse kept shipping to Cape Town. It seems they became more and more attracted to each other. Eventually Jesse proposed marriage. It's not surprising that she accepted. After all marriage was a way out of South Africa and an escape from the Apartheid which was enforced with brute force at the time. I listened in complete silence as Jesse ran all the scenarios down to me. He went on to tell me how he picked her up at a house party in Cape Town. This particular house catered to seafarers of color stopping off in Cape Town. During their stay many of the off duty crew met there for fun and games. An older lady ran the show and managed to keep everything under control at all times. The White South African Police knew well what was going on. Sometimes they dropped in to check out the situation. All the other Seamen just enjoyed the hospitality including the fun and games. When sailing time came it was a casual so long to the girls and see them next trip.

Not so for Jesse. He had fallen in love and would propose to his Juhl on the next trip. His fellow shipmates tried their damnedest to get him to change his mind. They advised him to get to know her better. They pleaded with him all the way from Cape Town to New Orleans and back again. But all of their pleas fell on deaf ears. Jesse had a mind of his own. He was one of the first crew members ashore after the ship docked in Cape Town. He met up with Juhl at the house. She told Jesse they had to have a heart to heart talk. She opened up and revealed all the skeletons in her closet. She told Jesse all about the men she picked up at the party house, about the rich, White men she picked up when working at a local resort hotel. They paid dearly for her favors. She told Jesse she was leveling with him because she didn't want him to marry her knowing he loved her, but not knowing about her loose morals. She would accept his proposal if he still wanted to marry her. Juhl would leave all of her notorious past behind in Cape Town and settle down with him in America to a life of decency and respectability. She sounded so sincere that Jesse was willing to forgive her. She even promised never to show up at the party house again. While Juhl was telling him these things, Jesse kept flipping a mental coin which kept coming up heads.

Jesse and Juhl had some red tape to cut through before their marriage was approved. She went through background checks from both the South African and United States governments before she was issued a passport and exit visa to America. They were able to marry and complete the paperwork before Jesse's ship sailed to Durban. Jesse took a trip off after returning to the States.

◆   ◆   ◆

Juhl flew out of South Africa and met him in New York as Mrs. Jesse Davis. They would live in New York instead of Louisiana. They settled in Hempstead on Long Island where Jesse had other close relatives. He dug into his savings to make a down payment on a three bedroom home. They had quite a honeymoon. Juhl met all his relatives in New York then they took a trip to Plaquemine, Louisiana. In his nearly two months off, they really made the rounds. Juhl looked on in awe. She had a house full of new furniture, a new family, and she would never have to see another Apartheid sign again. At 27 she seemed to have everything at her beck and call. She and Jesse even took turns in the kitchen. Juhl praised him for being a better cook than she was.

Just before Jesse shipped out again he brought in one of his female cousins to live with Juhl. Jesse hoped moving his cousin in would help Juhl adjust to her new surroundings. Jesse called Juhl aside and told her about what he expected from his wife while he was gone. He told her to feel free to go out and enjoy herself, and he hoped she would make new friends. Juhl was free to visit Manhattan to meet more people if she wanted to but when he returned home, he expected his house to be in order.

I had been listening without comment while sipping my beer then I glanced at the picture of Juhl above his bed and saw what a glamorous woman she was. I told Jesse he should have gotten his cousin to make the rounds with her or to help her find a part-time job to keep her active. He said that would come later. Our conversation about Juhl then ended. I wished them both the best. Jesse thanked me for listening and with a sad look on his face, asked me not to mention this conversation to other crew members. I promised him I would not betray his trust. I lapsed into a few moments of silence as I thought about the freedom of movement he was giving his wife. I was afraid he was waving a green light in front of her which could some day bring disaster.

◆   ◆   ◆

After drinking we both went to the Crew Mess for night lunch. We skipped the ham and instead had bologna and cheese on toast along with fruit punch. Several guys from the Deck Department and the wipers from the Engine Department came in. One of them thanked Jesse and complimented him on the peach pie at lunch. I was happy to see the crew mellowing out again. As we went our separate ways turning in for the night I realized that Jesse and I would remain the best of friends.

13

WAR ZONE—PART 2

We dropped anchor at Vung Tau and I was relieved to learn there would be shore leave. I would go ashore to see what was going on in this small resort village. Unlike Cam Ranh Bay, I saw no Vietnamese fishermen passing the stern of the ship in their small motor boats. There was something different about the village of Vung Tau at the mouth of the Mekong River. It was a bustle of activity with obvious signs of prosperity.

Just before lunch, the duty schedule went up. Knowing I had my job to cover, I didn't care about the early and mid-afternoon launches. I decided on the launch leaving the ship at 18:30 giving me time to clean up after dinner. The town was nearer than it looked from the ship and the launch had us ashore in a short while. All the gang was there. I was the only one in the group who was full of anxiety as to what the place would be like. All the others had been there before except Dale and Jake, and they had developed a more easy-going attitude about their travels.

◆　　◆　　◆

The Grand Hotel patio had a lively atmosphere. There were a few civilians there among the American and Australian Military personnel. Vietnamese women were available also. In Colonial times Vung Tau was known as Cape St. Jacques by the French. The bar in the Grand Hotel still had a French feel to it. Until you paid attention to the local people you might think you were in Marseille. Later we all went to a bar where the ladies were giving us all kinds of attention. They were also hustling drinks. Bruce, Charlie, Jesse, and Bob decided to stay awhile and play it by ear. I spoke in French to one of the girls as sort of a test case and she answered me in fluent French. This was quite a surprise. Many of the young Vietnamese didn't speak French but rather stuck to their own language. My own knowledge of the language is limited. Anytime I have the opportunity to converse with someone with more knowledge of French than I have, I grab it. She also spoke faltering English. Although she was a hustler this girl could charm the boots off any diplomat. Her name was Alice ("Aleece"). Alice may speak French and have a French name, but she was as Vietnamese as they come. After all, what's in a name?

My shipmates had another round and left in search of a different social climate. They hoped to find girls they had known from other voyages to Vung Tau. I told them I would meet them back at the landing where we would all go back on the same launch.

Alice and I continued our conversation. I found her so interesting that I stayed in her company until launch time.

We talked about many things including my childhood struggles growing up during the Great Depression and my travels around the world. She seemed impressed. She told of her experiences as a child growing up in the countryside during the waning years of French Colonialism and the War period. I gathered she was of the peasant class but had managed to lift herself up by the boot straps. I managed to steer the conversation clear of politics. Soon it was time for me to say "a demain" or "until tomorrow."

There was no romance this evening just a platonic evening full of interesting conversation and charming hospitality. I found that I liked Alice in spite of her job. She was a bar hustler and that was her gig. Entertaining me in her own way she never forced me to do anything I didn't want to do.

◆   ◆   ◆

It was quiet aboard ship the next morning. I went through routine duties. Several times I went out on deck to take in the tropical background until the intense heat drove me back inside.

By 18:30 we were back on the launch going ashore. I went back to the bar to find Alice. Some of my shipmates found their girlfriends from previous trips. Alice and I shared a delicious noodle soup. We then sat together over drinks for several hours conversing in both French and English. She had to correct my French more often than I had to correct her English. We had another enjoyable evening. When it came time to say "au revoir," I just gave her a hug and a kiss, walked out the door, and made my way to the landing. I refused to feel sentimental. I thought of Alice in a positive way. If only she could change jobs. She spoke three languages, fluent in two of them, with another type of job she could go far.

◆   ◆   ◆

The next morning some American Army personnel came aboard ship to serve as guards as we transited the river on our way to Saigon, now known as Ho Chi Minh City. Other than a few warning shots, the trip up river went without incident. Soon we were docked at Pier 3 in Saigon's Khanh Hoi district. It was just before 11:00. I could see from all the scenery coming into port that Saigon was a cultural world removed from the rest of Vietnam. I would later observe that the government buildings, hotels, downtown clubs, and restaurants had a strong French feel to their designs. In contrast, its Notre Dame Cathedral was built in gothic style architecture. I finally understood why Saigon was called the "Paris of the Orient." It rightfully deserved such a title.

Soon the ship was cleared for all off duty crew members to go ashore. I had to laugh at the way we all rushed down the gangway like a pack of wolves on the prowl. Many of the crew had been to Saigon before. They went to renew old friendships with girls and pick up where they last left off.

Bruce gave us the go ahead to take a meal or two off as long as one of our working partners would cover. I pointed to Charlie, telling him to go ahead. I would cover both dinner tonight and breakfast the next morning. When I told him that, he was one happy old timer. I considered it payback for all the times Charlie covered for me. He immediately went to our room, cleaned up, and dressed in one of his summer suits. He was headed down the gangway to meet up with a young girlfriend he knew from a previous voyage to Saigon. Jesse worked dinner and breakfast for K.O.

Kevin O'Keefe had been talking about his girlfriend in Saigon since the ship went under Military Sealift Command (M.S.C.). I would finally meet her after dinner. The few officers that came for dinner were in just as much of a hurry as I was to get out of the Mess Hall. I went ashore at 18:30 to check out the situation. I still had five hours before curfew.

I found the places I was to frequent in Saigon very conveniently located. Just about all of them were in walking distance. I walked around the corner from Pier 3 and saw a strip of bars. Two of the bars struck my fancy, *The Olympic* and *Ly Ly* ("Lee Lee"). Both were crowded but *Ly Ly* was less packed so I settled there for a drink. I ordered a tropical punch made with rum. It hit the spot. Looking down the bar I saw some of the Deck Department guys with their girls. We exchanged nods as I was leaving.

I returned to *The Olympic* and ordered a beer. Someone yelled my name. I looked around and saw K.O. sitting with his girlfriend at a nearby table. He called me over and introduced us using her Western name, Dena Ho. She was a very attractive Chinese girl who lived in Saigon's Chinese community of Cholon.

I left K.O. and Dena to enjoy each other's hospitality and went back to my own table. One of the young girls passed by and gave me an inviting smile. I called her over asking her if she spoke French. She said no and left my table heading for the back room. When she came back, an older woman, who I guessed to be in her early thirties, was with her. The girl introduced her as Lan and told me that she spoke French. I was in business. Lan would be my friend for the rest of our stay in Saigon. We chatted switching between French and English. I was nervous about staying ashore the first night in port. I explained that I wanted to meet her again the next night when I would be better prepared to spend the night ashore. She said she'd be there. I would condition myself for the next night come what may.

I was up early the next morning bringing the milk, juice, and fresh fruit from the chill box to the refrigerator in the Saloon Mess. Charlie had no need to worry. I had everything under control. After breakfast was served I took care of both of our cleanup jobs too. I didn't have time to join the guys in the Deck and Engine Departments for the 10:00 coffee break. They spent this time swapping stories about their adventures ashore.

On our second day in port I decided to skip my usual nap and take a motorbike taxi tour of Saigon instead. Some of the businesses were closed for siesta time. That was okay with me. I wasn't planning on shopping so soon. After all, we expected to be in Saigon for at least five more days. My tour guide took me to To Do ("Too-doe") Street, one of the main drags in Saigon. It was another strip of bars and clubs patronized mostly by American Military personnel on R&R from the field. These bars and clubs catered to an almost all White clientele so I decided to test the situation. I was served in all four bars and restaurants I tested. I was extended courteous treatment by the personnel on duty. In several cases the working girls were aloof when it came to socializing. After a peek in the lounges of the Majestic and Continental hotels, I decided it was time to return to the environs of Khanh Hoi where I was the night before. I had noticed that a number of Black American servicemen frequented the bars there. Most of the White patrons were civilians working on government contracts or crew members on ships in the harbor. Khanh Hoi and the bars within that district were under heavier patrol by the American MPs than those on To Do Street.

Most of the girls working in the Khanh Hoi district were either Vietnamese or Cambodian, but I saw one Black girl in *Ly Ly*. Her dark skin and straight black hair made her a real stand-out. As I approached her table the young White Army officer she was sitting with gave me a dirty look. I apologized for intruding and told the girl I was only curious about her ethnic background. She smiled and, speaking in heavily-accented English, told me that she was the daughter of a Vietnamese mother and a Senegalese father. She was a carryover from the days when the French Foreign Legionnaires were stationed in French Indo-China. I complimented her Vietnamese attire. Her boyfriend kept one arm around her shoulder and managed to force a smile and a handshake when he found that I wasn't trying to steal his girlfriend. I bid them both a good afternoon and left the bar.

I would not return to *The Olympic* until after dinner. Nor would I have any more beer until then. No mixing business with pleasure. On my break I went across from where the ship was docked to have a Coke. I met an older couple who ran a kind of patio concession stand just outside their home. They sold mostly beer and sodas, along with a few goodies, to Seamen who didn't want to frequent the strip. They were called Mamasan and Papasan. After all, they were the proud parents of 14 children. Their oldest son was in the Vietnamese Army.

Coming back off the ship after serving dinner I saw the Purser and Radio Officer. They were both carrying packages resulting from a recent shopping spree. I was thinking how nice it was they had skipped dinner. The Third Mates and Chief Mate Sully also skipped dinner. With so few officers to serve I was done quickly and on my way ashore. As I was leaving Pier 3 to turn the corner I saw Mamasan sitting out front with four of her children catching a late afternoon breeze. She smiled and acknowledged my greeting. I was moving on. Lan was waiting for me at *The Olympic*.

As I entered I saw Charlie sitting with his girl. He had left the ship a few minutes ahead of me. Bob and Jesse said hello and so did their girls. *The Olympic* would be the meeting place during our stay in Saigon. Bruce came in later but returned to the ship before curfew. Dale, Jake, and Ken were all on To Do Street. K.O. and Dena had already retired to their own corner of the world.

Lan and I continued getting acquainted with each other. We talked and drank, carefully avoiding the topic of politics. She didn't hustle me as much as I expected her to. I knew she was in business and was working for the bar but she treated me as fair as the house rules would allow. She was also teaching me some conversational French. We hit it off really well. I was willing to later give her a handsome tip. As Bob was on his way to the men's room, he heard us conversing in French. He burst out laughing. I suggested he go back to his girl or wherever he started from. He signaled Bruce and Charlie saying they had a Black Frenchman in the house. He was getting drunk but Lan and I paid him no mind. I liked Bob as a shipmate but as a Bos'n and leader of men he sometimes stepped out of line by saying the wrong things at the wrong times and showing his own ignorance. For once, Jesse was the best-behaved in the bar. He was nursing his drinks and sitting there all lovey-dovey with his girl. I was happy to see that and hoped that he would keep it up until the end of the voyage.

Curfew was drawing near, a blessing in disguise for those of us staying ashore. Each of us would go our separate way. Lan and I took separate taxis to her place. I considered it a bit odd but I didn't question it. I just complied with the rules she set. She had a small but nice place complete with mosquito netting over the bed. I noticed a picture of an American soldier on her dresser. She was very truthful about everything although I tried not to push the point. She confessed that her Army friend was in the field. He had just left two days before we arrived. I figured he wouldn't be back to Saigon before we sailed and I wouldn't have to worry about him storming in and shooting the place up. We settled in for a nice exciting evening.

Returning to the ship the next morning I thought about a practice I had heard about where Seamen paid their girlfriends to stay out of the bars while they were away. That way they thought they would have no worry about her fooling around with other guys during his absence. How naïve could they be? Sometimes these guys would be gone for months at a time. The average one of those girls could make a mint working the bars during this time in addition to the money he paid her to be faithful. C'est la vie.

At mail call Bruce handed me two letters, one from Betty and one from Adrian. Betty wrote about how she enjoyed meeting my shipmates at the party she and I hosted at her home. She insisted I say hello to my shipmates for her. She also told of daily life like getting her car out of the shop. Adrian on the other hand wrote a lengthier letter. She thanked me again for all the help I had given her. She found a larger two bedroom apartment just down the street from her parent's home. Her little boy was well and into everything. Larry, Dottie, and Breaux sent their regards and looked forward to seeing me on my next trip through New Orleans. Before ending her letter she warned me to be careful and try to come back all in one piece. Reading the letters made my day.

That day after dinner when I reached *The Olympic*, Lan had a surprise for me. She fixed me a dinner of fish and rice with a side dish of vegetables and peppers. The peppers were so hot I drank down most of my beer while she went to get me a glass of water. The dinner was delicious especially the fish. I ordered another beer to wash down the peppers.

At Lan's place we talked awhile engaging in general conversation. She offered me water from a jug. The beer had not quite quenched my thirst. The spicy dinner was still churning inside me but that didn't stop us from having a beautiful evening. After she fixed her hair and changed into her night clothes she looked just as lovely as the first night I met her at *The Olympic*.

The next morning I decided to splurge on several overseas phone calls. I went to the U.S.O. and found it jammed with servicemen. Surprisingly, I still got my call through. Unlike most of the Military men, who reversed their calls, I paid for mine up front. The timing was good. It was 10:00 AM in Saigon which meant it was early evening the night before on the East Coast in America. I talked with one of my sisters in South Carolina and Adrian in New Orleans. They both warned me to be careful. Adrian thanked me for the gift of silk. She was having a dress made right away. I was happy to find out she had received it already. I mailed it from an Army Post Office in Qui Nhon.

"I can hardly believe I'll be wearing a Japanese silk dress," Adrian said.

"You can wear it the next time I take you out on the town."

"Everyone at the cafeteria asks about you from time to time."

"Tell them all 'hello' for me."

She laughed and asked, "How's the weather in Saigon?"

"Much too hot!" Before we hung up I told her, "Keep on looking good. Let's stay in touch."

After talking with Adrian I rushed back to the ship to set up for lunch. Several officers came in to tell me they would not be in for lunch. They were all decked out in their tropical best and on their way to To Do Street. Five more at lunch told me they would be skipping dinner.

"Have a good evening," I told them with a smile.

I couldn't believe my luck in having so few people to serve. Charlie had overheard them and was grinning from ear to ear. I told him I would cover both meals for him since Bruce had already given us the okay. He declined taking off for lunch but rather took a nap for two hours and took dinner off.

On Saturday afternoon I asked Charlie to cover for me at the next lunch so I could attend Church services at Notre Dame Cathedral.

"You kidding me?" he asked.

"No," I said, "I want to take advantage of being where there's a cathedral and take another look around town before we sail."

Not too many shipmates made time for church in Saigon.

"Take off and don't worry about it," Charlie said as he headed for our room and an afternoon nap. He had begun to look haggard and showing his age. All of those young ladies were tearing him up.

A few minutes after 16:00 when I was setting up for dinner, Charlie walked by on his way ashore. He was wearing a blue tropical shirt, gray trousers, and a pair of Stacy Adams shoes. He had replaced his usual straw hat for a gray summer hat. The nap had done him good. As he walked out of the Galley toward the gangway I told him to tell Lan I would see her later. K.O. was covering dinner for Jesse. He told me Jesse was sober so far and handed me a bowl of chili and beans. I went to the steam table and got a scoop of rice then shook a little Tabasco sauce over the works. I got a glass of iced tea with lemon and sat down to eat. I normally would eat dinner after the officers' meal, but in port I ate before so I could rush ashore after cleanup. While I was eating in the Crew Mess, Bruce brought me some good news. The Captain and the Chief Engineer would be having dinner ashore. I was having a ball with so many officers not having dinner aboard, but wait until the following week at sea. They would all be there and I would have to really earn my salary for all three meals. But for now I would just enjoy these good times while they lasted.

I stopped by for a short chat with Mamasan and Papasan and bought a soda to finish washing down my chili dinner.

"Girlfriend?" Mamasan asked as she pointed in the direction of the bars.

I guess she knew I was on my way there. She only sold light refreshments and hardly any girls were available. The only girls I ever saw there were her older daughters, who were definitely off limits. They were only good for a chat or to serve the customers. The Merchant Seamen and a few Army guys who dropped by were mostly older men who were married and not looking for girls, but just wanted to drink, socialize, and stay faithful to the wives they left behind. Sometimes a few broke curfew by being out after 23:00 but the MPs didn't push it too far since they lived just across the way less than five minutes from the ship. Seemingly they ran quite a profitable business, also it was a no nonsense business always keeping things in line.

I stopped in *Ly Ly* to sit awhile with K.O. and Dena. K.O. was in his glory just like he would be all through the Orient. I briefly observed Dena. She looked more like she had just signed a contract with some big time modeling agency rather than cavorting in some bar on a Saigon strip. The other girls would watch her with seemingly envious eyes. In the bar she stood out. The younger girls were attractive, but many of them were on the short side. These Vietnamese and Cambodian girls looked to be in their early twenties. K.O. told me that Dena was 32, three years older than he was, but her lovely face and statuesque build brought roving eyes from the male customers whenever she strolled around the bar. She was an asset to the boss.

I had exchanged enough money to carry me through the weekend. I had a sufficient amount of piastres for the next two days. That way I wouldn't have to carry American green money ashore and get involved with the black market.

I went bar hopping in a few other bars in Khanh Hoi. Most of them were crowded, a few were half empty, but all with customers enjoying themselves on a Saturday night. When I went into *The Olympic* all the gang was there. Lan drew up several tables so that we all could sit together for Saturday night fun.

On Sunday morning in Saigon I helped serve breakfast and Charlie told me to take off. He would take care of lunch as he had promised. I left the ship at about 10:00. I wore my blue summer shirt, matching blue trousers, and newly shined black shoes. I knew full well they would be dusty again before I returned to the *Marine Charger*. As I took my time wandering down To Do Street I glanced at the bars and shops but passed them all by. This tree-lined street was a sight to behold. I kept walking and just outside the Continental Hotel, a Vietnamese passerby suggested I may want to visit the American Embassy. It was a modern structure looking good and well fortified. I was satisfied watching it from a distance. I had no desire or need to go inside. A short distance away, I found myself face to face with what I really came ashore for in the first place. I was right at the doors of Notre Dame Cathedral just in time for the 11:00 Mass. I looked in awe at these people of diverse backgrounds coming together to worship. The cathedral was crowded but I was ushered in about halfway down the isle. I went through the rituals without a hitch, in spite of the Mass being conducted in a foreign language. Notre Dame inside and outside looked about like the average Catholic cathedral. The large crowd of Vietnamese there came as a surprise since the population of Vietnam is only 20 percent Catholic. I must say I left Mass feeling humble at the way I was received. I'll never forget.

◆   ◆   ◆

As I took a casual walk back down To Do Street I met an African American girl, a real Soul sister. She had just left the Majestic Hotel. Whether she had been there to wine and dine or whatever, I didn't ask. I introduced myself and she did likewise. Her name was Mary Brown and she was from Norfolk, Virginia.

"I know some people there," I told her. "In fact I was there just a few months ago. What brought you to Saigon?"

"I'm a Nurse in the U.S. Army. I'm stationed at the hospital here in Saigon."

I was moved by her nonchalant manner. Here I was in the company of an Army lieutenant who considered it no big thing. She was dressed in civilian clothes. One of her fellow nurses wanted off so she was returning to the hospital at 13:00 to stand by. I was not coming on to Mary, but I had to make my point by inviting her to see the ship. Here I was an entry rating Messman strolling onboard with this First Lieutenant, Registered Nurse. As for the crew, it would blow their minds to bits and pieces. Mary hesitated at first. It was almost 12:30 and she had plans to meet a dear friend for coffee before she went on duty at the hospital. He would be disappointed if she didn't show up. I understood, but promised her it would be a whirlwind tour of the ship. She reluctantly agreed. We taxied to the ship. As we approached the gangway a young Army duty guy wanted to know who Mary was and what business she had coming to the ship. She took out her Armed Forces I.D. card and handed it to him. With a surprised look on his face he gave her a snappy salute and handed her back the card. She returned it to her purse and the guard waved us on. My chest must have gone out a mile. That Black gal was looking good. She was wearing a tropical dress with red flowers and a brown wide brim straw hat.

"Let me take off my shoes," she said as we started up the ladder.

She removed her high heels to avoid tripping. We went up the gangway and there was Sully talking to one of the Third Mates and the AB on watch. While Mary put her shoes back on, I explained things to Sully and asked his permission to show Mary around. We just wanted to go on a quick tour of the Bridge and Mess decks. We would skip the Engine Room and Crew's Quarters. Sully agreed providing I stay with her the whole time she was aboard. I would take full responsibility for her safety. I understood how particular ship officials felt about visitors especially in a War Zone. Mary being another American, and an Army officer, made her an exception. One thing's for sure, I would not make it a habit asking for such a favor.

As we approached the ladder leading to the Bridge, Mary took off her shoes again. We met Lester who was on his way ashore. I introduced him to Mary and asked him to go to the Bridge with us. As an Able-Bodied Seaman he knew much more about navigation than I did. He was happy to oblige and the three of us spent a whole five minutes looking around the Bridge. After thanking and bidding a good-afternoon to Lester, Mary and I headed for the Crew and Saloon Mess Halls. Like all of our guests, Mary thought the menu selections were awesome.

Charlie would be on his way ashore soon along with K.O. and Jesse. Bruce and Juan were chatting in Bruce's office. I introduced Mary to all of them. They hardly knew what to say. I told Charlie I would take care of dinner. He thanked me and then looked Mary over.

Mary and I peeked into the sleeping quarters and she remarked on how small the space was for two people to share.

"We share the room, but not the beds," I told her.

She burst out laughing saying, "I hope not!"

We walked back out on deck and to the gangway. Most of the crew were already ashore, but those still aboard were all eyes. I could read their minds. They all wanted to know who Mary was. That happened a lot when an American woman came aboard an American ship in a foreign port. I enjoyed the many stares she drew.

We went across the pier to visit awhile with Mamasan and Papasan. While there, Martinjak passed us by heading downtown along with Jim Long the Third Engineer. They both waved while giving Mary a curious look. Mary made it clear that she would soon be going on duty and that meant no alcohol for her. We sat for a round of Cokes and she complimented us for running such a clean ship. I told her the Captain would have it no other way. Within a half an hour I was escorting Mary back to the hospital. She wanted to stay longer, but duty called. As we left, Bob and several of his Ordinary Seamen came up on their way back to the ship from a shopping trip. I made all of the introductions.

"How the hell did you meet Buzz?" Bob asked her.

"None of your business," I answered half jokingly.

That drew a big laugh from Mary. Without a doubt, she was really enjoying all of the attention she was getting from the ship's crew. Stationed in Saigon at 25 years of age, single, and good looking, Mary had many men she could have spent time with. I felt humbled that she chose to visit the ship with me. When I saw her back to the hospital she invited me to sit awhile. I had to beg forgiveness explaining that I had just visited a medical facility in Vietnam several weeks earlier and didn't feel up to seeing another one so soon. From what I heard some of her patients were in bad shape.

Mary asked me to meet her later at a place near To Do Street where the Army officers met. At first I wondered how it would be with her fellow officers, then on second thought I realized it would be no big deal since I was a civilian. There shouldn't be any hassles about her fraternizing with me. I would insist on her having dinner with me knowing full well our date would be platonic and nothing more. After awhile I said so long to Mary and her coworkers and made it back across town to Pier 3. I would stay aboard Sunday night skipping both *Ly Ly* and *The Olympic*.

After serving dinner I took my own dinner of steak, fries, and green peas to the Crew Mess and pigged myself. Then I took some ice cream from the freezer. I thought about Mary as I grabbed two backdated *Stars and Stripes* newspapers to read before going to bed.

◆   ◆   ◆

Come Monday between lunch and dinner, I decided it was time I satisfied my curiosity about a place called "Soul Alley." I had heard about it from some Military and ex-Military guys who did tours of duty in Vietnam. I wanted to see it for myself. I got a street wise Vietnamese man to show me the way. I hitched a ride with him on his scooter. When we reached Soul Alley I was surprised to find that it looked much like other parts of Saigon I had traveled through. I stopped into one of the party houses known as a hootch and found that it was being patronized by young, Black soldiers and their Vietnamese women. There were several White and Latino soldiers in the crowd as well, but mostly Blacks. The others were trying to see how Black they could act in order to fit in, imitating Black slang as some would do in the States. As I approached the patio they pegged me right away as being a civilian. I guess they could tell I was an outsider due to my age and the way I carried myself. They offered me a beer which came in handy on a hot afternoon. I started a conversation about coming to Vietnam on a Merchant cargo ship. I could tell by their battle weary looks that they were in from the field for a little R&R. The ones that told me they were stationed in Saigon seemed more relaxed. Some were in the company of women while others were just hanging out carrying on general conversation and drinking. One of them was talking with his girl who was nursing a mixed-race baby. I was doing okay sipping my beer when one of them offered me a joint. I declined. I could smell the pot all around. They were mellow young dudes. Some told me how they had been getting harassed by the MPs. I advised them to keep their cool and stay out of trouble, reminding them that they were in a War Zone and to a certain extent living under Military law. They kind of looked up to me as an elder. They told me how drugs were available in the bars of Saigon and other parts of Vietnam. We chatted for almost two hours. I declined a second offer of pot but had drunk three of their beers. I singled out one of them who seemed to be in charge of the house. I handed him ten dollars in piastres to contribute to restocking their alcohol supply. He didn't want to accept it but I insisted. As I got up to leave I again warned them about being in a War Zone. I told them to try to have a safe trip back to the U.S.A. when their tours of duty ended in Vietnam. One of them arranged for a scooter to take me back to the ship. Before I could climb aboard, I saw two MPs standing a few yards away.

"Oh, no!" I said to myself as a trembling fear came over me.

I feared I would be busted and end up in Long Binh Jail ("L.B.J."). The MPs stared at us. Both of them were young, White soldiers. They seemed to be debating whether to check out the situation. Silence fell over the crowd. I decided to make the first move by telling my Vietnamese driver to go straight toward them and then stop. I had already thanked the soldiers for their hospitality. They invited me to come again. As my driver and I approached the MPs, I decided to be extra polite to distract their attention from the soldiers at the corner who were watching it all.

"Evening Officers," I greeted them. "Hot day."

Neither of them returned my greeting. Instead one of them asked to see my identification. After reading my Z-card and learning of my civilian status, they became friendlier.

"What brought you to the neighborhood?" one of them asked.

"Curiosity," I replied.

"Avoid the Alley," the other one warned. "It's real trouble."

"Are you lost?" the first MP asked.

"The scooter driver is taking me back to Pier 3 where my ship is docked," I assured him.

I was happy to see them turn and walk away from the hootch. As I left the scene my parting remarks with them were the same as with the soldiers at the party.

"Have a safe trip back to the U.S.A. at the end of your tour."

"You too," was their answer as they walked slowly back to their jeep.

I visited Saigon seven more times before its fall in 1975, but never again did I visit Soul Alley. It would be etched in my memory for a lifetime.

After paying the driver I went back aboard. I served dinner enjoying the absenteeism of so many of my customers. I went back ashore to have another enjoyable evening and night with Lan but I kept thinking about Soul Alley and all the young lives involved.

◆   ◆   ◆

The next morning I decided to make another overseas call. This one was to Judy back in Sydney. We were in nearly the same time zone. I reached her just before she left for work. As we chatted she said I was insane for being in Vietnam and thanked me for the gifts I had mailed her. She said nothing had changed in Sydney. Her friends asked about me often. She wanted to know when I would return. I told her I couldn't say just when, but hopefully soon. I suggested we keep in touch.

"Yes, you do that," she said laughing.

At the time I did owe her a letter and couldn't make any excuses about a busy schedule which wasn't true.

"Be careful," she said as we ended our conversation. "Love you."

"As if I didn't love you," I replied.

We laughed and said our goodbyes. That call really made my day. I would make my way to the U.S.O. on other trips to Saigon to take advantage of such a convenient and inexpensive facility. Little did I know it would be ten years before I made my way back to Australia.

◆   ◆   ◆

After lunch I went across the way to sit awhile with Mamasan and Papasan. A few customers were sitting out front with Mamasan when I arrived. They were from another American ship docked nearby. It would not be long before we all would have some unexpected entertainment.

Jesse came by with a Vietnamese girlfriend, not his regular girl, but one he had picked up on the corner. He was trying to get her aboard ship. Mamasan, who was not missing a trick, saw him hand this girl 20 dollars. Jesse was half drunk at the time. We all knew the young American Army guard would wave Jesse on through but he would turn her around. That's just what he did.

Jesse cursed the guard, who was merely carrying out orders, and staggered on aboard the ship. The guard then turned to the streetwalker and said "Didi!" meaning shove off. She obeyed his orders without question walking away with the 20 dollars tucked securely in her bra and a smile on her face. She was happy to have gotten something for nothing. Mamasan told Papasan who had just come outside, what had just happened. They of course spoke in Vietnamese between uncontrolled laughter. The customers from the nearby ship also began laughing.

It was obvious that everybody there enjoyed the show. The guard walked back to the checkpoint with a look on his face that said "mission accomplished."

◆   ◆   ◆

After about an hour of visiting, I returned to the ship to write some letters. When my dinner duties were done, I was off to meet up with Mary and her friends at the restaurant and bar downtown. I wanted to dress accordingly knowing well that I might be the only civilian in the group. I wore my gray silk mohair suit with a white shirt and blue tie. When I met them I noticed that none of them were in uniform which made me feel more comfortable. There were eight people in the party including myself. I was Mary's guest, and then there were three other couples all from the hospital staff and all officers: first lieutenants and captains. We went through several rounds of drinks. It was only 19:30 and I had no intentions of making any rounds in Khanh Hoi that evening. Curfew was still far away. Then it was time to sit down to dinner. We all ordered. Mary had been drinking what she called a weak scotch. She switched to gin and tonic as she began to let her hair down. I never lied about my job title. Some of my fellow shipmates did. They would tell strangers that they were a Mate or an Engineer when they were only an AB or an Electrician or some other non-licensed personnel.

At dinner I was asked my job title. Without hesitation I told the male guest who asked the question that I was a Messman or waiter in the Officer's Mess, or Saloon Mess as they call it. Mary then spoke up by saying I keep the officers happy. There were only three of us Blacks in the party. The other woman was one of Mary's fellow nurses. She wore a shy smile and said little. The five Whites, three men and two ladies, were the life of the party; especially after the alcohol started setting in. When I told them I shipped from San Francisco they started questioning me about Berkeley and the University of California in relation to the anti-Vietnam War demonstrations. I told them I only go to Berkeley to use the U.C. Bancroft Undergraduate Library. They were impressed. It seems they were trying to set me up for a question and answer session. I shied away from questions about the ship's movement for security reasons. Then Mary came to my rescue telling them to lay off so many personal questions.

"Talk about some other action going on both Stateside and elsewhere," she said.

We embraced and kissed on that one. I was really enjoying Mary and was happy to have met her. I found her to be at times an officer and a lady like she was the day she visited the ship or the bitch on wheels if you incurred her wrath. She could also use some lumberjack's language when getting her head bad. She was by no means alone. Some others in the party didn't do too badly for themselves in that respect. I got compliments on my suit from one of the men. I could tell he'd been around. He told me my suit was made by a Japanese tailor and my shoes were strictly East Coast. He was quite an expert on clothing but I was hardly impressed. All of us passed on dessert. They just couldn't figure out how I could have such knowledge of world events and with my intellectual pursuits why hold such a menial job? I told them it was by choice for now. Later I might have other plans after another trip around the world. I had to make one more grandstand for the evening. When the meal was over, the men reached in their pockets to pay the tab.

"No way," I yelled across the table. "Keep your hands away from your pockets and your purses. This Messman has it all covered."

Mary laughed so loud that she could be heard halfway down To Do Street. I reached in my pocket and pulled out nearly a hundred dollars in piastres. I learned the seafood dinner had come to far less for the eight of us than I had expected. I paid the whole tab plus a handsome tip to the well mannered Cambodian waiter. I put the left over money back in my pocket. I proved a point. My job on the ship was menial but my salary was definitely not.

Mary and I engaged in some private conversation. She gave me the names of some bar maids she knew back in Norfolk. I was to let them know she'd be back in five months. It was a deal. We talked about visiting and being stationed in a War Zone. It was not like being elsewhere, but was something a person just had to get used to. I thanked her for coming out with me. She was dating this guy but they weren't too serious. Then I told her half jokingly about the girls I left back in the States who I wanted the hell out of. But they didn't want the hell out of me as the old saying goes. The couple sitting next to us laughed out loud.

Mary laughed and said, "I know what you mean." She was really enjoying herself.

All the others in the party had warmed up to me and stopped the question and answer session. Just before 22:00 the party broke up. The medical officers would be returning to their living quarters. They all thanked me again for the treat and insisted that I look them up my next trip to Saigon. Mary said we'd get together again soon after she gave me a warm embrace and a kiss she really meant. I told her we must stay in touch but the way things happened it would be 19 years before we met again.

As planned, I bypassed the bars in Khanh Hoi as I taxied back to the ship. The next night there would be one more French lesson with Lan. In the meantime I was ready to hit the hay. It had been one long day. I bypassed the bar on the pier too. As I went up the gangway and on inside the ship I noticed some Vietnamese longshoremen on break. Alongside them stood two nice looking women who were also working on the cargo. They looked a little frail for such an occupation but I guess they managed to keep up.

The next morning at breakfast Sully asked, "How is your nurse friend getting along?"

"We went out to dinner at the Officer's Club last night," I told him.

"How did you pull that off?"

"It was an accident, nothing serious. I sure liked spending time doting on an American girl in Saigon," I told him.

Both the Second Mate and Martinjak, who saw me leave the ship with Mary, complimented me on my good taste. I poked my head into the Crew Mess just in time to hear Bob sounding the alarm about me running with nurses and other officers. One of his ABs wanted to know if the crew wasn't good enough for me to associate with. I laughed at them all. Jesse who was filling an order of country scrambled eggs, bacon, and potatoes in the Galley, rushed to the Crew Mess coming to my rescue.

"That man runs with whom he pleased," he said. "He owes you no explanation." He finished by telling them all, "Carry your ignorant asses!"

"Thank you," I told him and the case was dismissed as I returned to the Saloon Mess to finish serving breakfast.

On my three hour break between lunch and dinner, I took a nap for several hours. When I got up and went out on deck I saw Bruce and Charlie talking to one of the Army officers who supervised the cargo. Charlie told me I'd better make it good tonight ashore. When I asked him why he pointed to the gangway knowing what I would see there. The sailing board had been posted. We would sail the next morning at 08:00 for Sattahip, Thailand. It would have been nice to spend another weekend in Saigon, but it's sometimes good to let well enough alone. We had spent almost a week in Saigon, and a total of 29 days in the War Zone. Not bad bonus time! In Thailand at least we would not be in a War Zone. We would be free to move around more. In spite of all this freedom of movement a person could still get into trouble.

The night before departure just about all the crew who were not on duty went ashore. On my way ashore, after serving dinner, I stopped by Mamasan's place. She and Papasan had fixed snacks for us as a sort of going away gesture. It was nice of them, but I had to be on my way to *The Olympic*. After bidding them so long, I was off to meet Lan and the other girls at the bar. All my drinking buddies were also there for a final night in Saigon. The girls were really putting on their act, saying how much they would miss us. Lan told me she would miss me so much she would cry if she went to Pier 3 where the ship was docked. She said I would be forever on her mind until she sees me again. I told her I wished there was some way I could jump ship and move in with her. Who knows? I joked that I might just jump into the mouth of the Mekong River and swim back to Saigon. Suddenly we were both laughing at the lies we were telling. That's just what they were, lies from both of our lips. The next day Lan would be moving on with her life in Saigon and I would be moving on with my life sailing far away. I would spend the night ashore and once more enjoy the pleasure of her company. After that I would hand over all of my left over piastres, which amounted to almost 40 dollars and move on with my adventure.

◆   ◆   ◆

In spite of setting sail half way through breakfast, we didn't offer an early or late breakfast time. All of the crew and officers were on top of their jobs in spite of the occasional unwanted hangover. There were no rumors of bad behavior. After breakfast I went out on deck to gaze around at what greenery I could see on the banks of the river. The American soldiers with their heavy artillery were seeing us out of the War Zone. They were mighty good to have around.

Thinking back on Saigon I looked on it as a fairly safe place to be, unlike other ports in Vietnam. I had heard about a restaurant being bombed. But with such a heavy Military presence, numbering about five hundred thousand in South Vietnam at the time, and Saigon being so heavily fortified, I felt safe while walking around in its downtown streets and nearby suburbs. Less than a year later the 1968 Tet Offensive would surely change my mind. As we left the War Zone behind the American guards left our ship and we went our separate ways. I returned time after time to Saigon over the years, each time reassessing that my views and opinions of Saigon were justified.

I read the *Stars and Stripes* after lunch before going for a nap and decided to wait and read the *Time Magazine* the next day before reaching Thailand. After dinner Martinjak brought me six beers from a case he picked up in Saigon. He had good contacts there. I thanked him as I put the beer in my locker. I already had some beer on ice for the after dinner get-together in our room. Charlie and I would host the gang who would be comparing sea stories on the differences between Saigon and Sattahip. I had never been to Thailand. I would be listening carefully to seek any beforehand information available. K.O. came in with a tall glass of Irish whiskey on the rocks. It was his way of enjoying a retreat from the Galley. By the time Jesse, Dale, and Jake squeezed in, the room was overfilled. Dale and Jake would be listening with all ears since they too had never been to Thailand before. Jesse dropped six beers in the cooler. Charlie was watching him like a hawk to see what condition he was in at the time and after a night of drinking, what condition he would be in to work breakfast the next morning.

"I'm alright," Jesse assured him.

He was upset because he couldn't reach his wife when he called home the day before. To hear him talk, Juhl shouldn't have been anywhere else when he decided to call. I remembered our recent conversation about the freedoms he offered her, but made no comment. Bob was standing in the doorway sipping a beer. He told Jesse it was no big deal. He called his wife several days ago and she wasn't in. Bob said he just kept trying until he reached her and then chewed her ass out for spending too much of his money. Laughter broke out. Jesse still had an irritated look on his face. K.O. refilled his whiskey and talked about Dena, the girl he left behind in Saigon. He said that he already missed her. She really treated him nice. We all had a good understanding of what he was feeling, but all good things must come to an end. K.O. could begin looking forward to seeing his Thai-Chinese girlfriend in Sattahip. All of the experienced Seamen agreed that the Thai girls were more relaxed than the girls in Vietnam. They are, as Jesse and K.O. said, a little more charming.

I interrupted to say, "I'll see."

Charlie repeated his sentiments of a few ports earlier. He would have a good time with the girls while passing through but he could hardly wait to get back to the true woman of his life back in Seattle. Another thing they all agreed on was that Thailand was not in a War Zone. There would be less stress and tension to worry about when going about daily rounds.

"Just be careful about being robbed," they cautioned.

We agreed to go ashore in groups or pairs especially to the smaller places outside the American Army base. In certain communities some taxis were not trustworthy. I was told some of them would pick you up, but instead of carrying you to your destination, they would take you to some waiting predators. They would rob you, beat you up, and leave you for dead. I listened carefully to their advice and made mental notes. I made the decision that I would still go ashore. I was not going to come all the way to the Gulf of Siam and stay aboard ship. I would go ashore at least two or three nights, come what may.

After swapping a few more sea stories all the gang drifted off to bed. Not much alcohol was left over to put back in the locker. The South China Sea would not be cruel to us. It was smooth sailing all the way to Sattahip.

14

THAILAND

My first day in Thailand would be low-keyed. It was a known fact that we would be there a few days so I decided to lie low the first night in port. After dinner, I went to one of the nearby Military clubs and managed to catch the end of happy hour. The prices of drinks and food were so cheap I ended up staying there for several more hours. The crew was friendly. Local Thai girls were there as well as American Army men. I sought information about the local surroundings as I mingled with both groups. Some of the girls were available for pick-up, but I held back until looking into the situation further. Before the evening was over I talked with one of the soldiers about a ride to Bangkok. It so happened that two of them were driving there in an Army vehicle on Sunday, just two days away. They said I was welcome to hitch a ride with them. No charge except to help out with the gas. The deal was set for Sunday morning so I said goodnight. It was late afternoon when I came to the club, but it was the black of night when I left.

Guards at the gate warned me that it would be dangerous walking the mile to the ship. Large snakes like King Cobras sometimes crossed the highway. I had been a few sheets to the wind but after that warning I sobered up in a hurry. Within ten minutes they had some base transportation to take me to the pier.

During my three-hour afternoon break I visited the nearby countryside. I hired a private taxi that looked trustworthy. He had a small statue of Buddha in the windshield. He drove me around as I watched some farmers at work tending their fields. Then we came to what looked like a pasture. I noticed a water buffalo grazing peacefully. Atop her back was a bird picking away at ticks, bugs, flies or whatever. I asked the driver to stop. This was a sight to observe. The water buffalo did not flinch. The bird kept on picking away and the water buffalo kept right on grazing. What some Thais later told me made sense. The birds were able to feed on the back of the water buffalo while at the same time helping her to get rid of unwanted parasites.

That night I joined the gang from the ship and went to town. At the bar there was a big party with girls galore. Many of them bore a striking resemblance to the ones we left behind in Saigon. A girl was available for anyone who wanted one. One girl, Chon, invited me to dinner at her home. After a few drinks I felt safe enough to accept her offer. Her place was just another shack but her attitude of "my house is your house" made me feel so welcome. I spent the night with her, enjoying myself so much I was almost late for work. Thanks to Charlie, everything was all set up when I rushed into the Saloon Mess. What a good partner.

My drinking buddies and I went back to the same club on Saturday. Chon was there and we repeated our performance of the night before. We painted the town but this time I was more sensible and got back to the ship in plenty of time.

◆   ◆   ◆

Sunday came and the two Army guys I was traveling to Bangkok with met me on the ship as planned at 10:00. Charlie had agreed to cover my duties for lunch and dinner and Bruce okayed the plan. With that settled, we were on our way to Bangkok. The driver, Dan, did most of the talking while Bill, who had a full Saturday night, catnapped in the back seat.

At Utapao Royal Air Force Base the big aircraft were an awesome sight. Being on a base little more than a stone's throw from the two Vietnams, I didn't dare take any photos and I asked very few questions. I felt relieved when we got out of that area.

Dan suggested we stop briefly at Pattaya Beach, a resort area on the way to Bangkok. The beach was overrun with tourists. Many were Americans and other Westerners. The ladies that were thinly clad in swimwear got all of our attention, including Bill in the backseat. We spent about an hour at Pattaya then drove non-stop to Bangkok. Dan was pointing out a few sights along the way. Some sights he didn't have to point out like the larger-than-life statue of Buddha sitting majestically on his throne. Seeing so many images of Buddha I guessed that the majority of the Thai were Buddhists. Then coming into the suburbs of Bangkok I noticed an unwelcome sight. I was ready to roll up the windows from what I saw. On the side of the road were long-legged, black spiders the length of the palm of my hand dangling from wires and poles. Dan said they were harmless, but I certainly didn't believe him. I had seen many spiders in both the U.S.A. and in other parts of the world, but none that size. I told him of hearing about cobras being spotted in those parts of Thailand. I wanted to know if I would see a tiger before we sailed again. He said tigers were mostly in northern Thailand quite a way away. That was a relief to know. The same would be true of panthers and wild boars.

We went on a tour of Bangkok including many clubs and hotels. Some of the hotels looked like those you'd find in Miami Beach. I was surprised to find out how cheap the rent was, just five dollars per night.

Dan was finally able to wake Bill up from his snooze in the back seat. Their girlfriends' place was just down the street. They invited me to come along. I declined in favor of seeing some more of Bangkok on my own like maybe a Buddhist temple or an open air market where I could bid for souvenirs. Dan agreed that he and Bill would meet me at a club two doors away from their girlfriends' place at 20:00 for the drive back to Sattahip. It was then just after 14:00 so I had about six hours to see more of the city.

After we split up, I went to one of the hotels and picked up a tour guide brochure. One of the girls at the desk was eager to give me all the information I needed. She called a taxi to take me to some souvenir shops and jewelry stores. I copied down the address and telephone number of the bar where I started from in order to meet back up with Dan and Bill. I didn't realize how large a city Bangkok was; moreover what a large population it had at that time. It numbered nearly two million people. Bangkok has quite a few canals, almost like being in Venice. I visited a houseboat. Quite a number of the city's population lived on houseboats. Having come all the way from the U.S.A. by ship I had no desire to spend any of my shore leave on the canals; I'd had enough water for awhile.

It was time to head for the shops. At one shop I bought five yards of Thai silk for Betty. How lovely she would look in that blue cocktail dress after the seamstress completed the job. I went on looking around. A person could spend a fortune in the shops of Bangkok with so much to choose from. I bought a jade ring for Adrian and one for myself. Jade was so inexpensive in Thailand it was a steal. Since I was getting low in baht, the Thai currency, it was time I checked my spending. That didn't stop me from window shopping. I went to a shop to find out about how expensive it was to purchase a pair of tailor-made shoes. The shopkeeper told me it wouldn't be very expensive and it wouldn't take very long either. My timing was off so he made a deal with me. He measured my feet. He would call in the exact measurements to a friend who had a shop in Sattahip. My shoes would be waiting there on Monday. I thanked him for making the arrangements.

Before making it to the other side of the city I noticed that there was a large population of Chinese in Bangkok. They were running quite a few of the businesses and enjoying a bit of prosperity. Feeling a bit hungry I went into a Chinese restaurant. Among the patrons, there were about as many tourists as there were local Chinese. As I sat down a waiter who spoke fluent English, came over to my table to help me read the menu. Some of it was written in English. I ordered a large bowl of Won Ton soup and some chicken fried rice. They loaded me up with both orders. After eating and sipping hot tea I paid the waiter, leaving him a handsome tip.

I took a taxi back where I started from, went into a large bar full of young people, and began to mix in. I ordered a Thai beer which tasted better than I thought it would. There was quite a bit of dancing going on. I danced with complete strangers. To my surprise not one girl I asked to dance turned me down. The small combo was working out. There were tourists from as far away as Australia and Hong Kong. The way it looked, both locals and tourists were enjoying themselves. I found a seat near a group of tourists about half way down the bar. They were from Burma and very friendly. I spent almost three hours there. I was in the middle of a slow dance with a young Thai lady when I got a tap on the shoulder. I turned around to see Dan and Bill. Time had passed me by. I asked them to have one beer with me before leaving the bar. Being the driver, Dan refused but accepted a Coke instead. Bill accepted a beer. We sat at the table with the five Burmese tourists, two men and three women. I was enjoying myself so much that I was hardly ready to leave Bangkok, but I had no choice. Duty would be calling early the next morning. I said so long to my table mates. One of the women who had been to the dance floor with me several times gave me a hug. I in turn gave her a buss on the cheek. The other two ladies also gave me hugs but I gave them no buss in respect to their husbands. I thanked the bartender for keeping my gifts and souvenirs tucked away and the three of us were on our way back to Sattahip.

Bill wasted no time curling up in the back seat. Dan assured me he was in good driving condition. He had caught a two hour nap in his girlfriend's bed. We carried on a fairly good conversation for nearly two hours about everything from Australia and New Zealand to New Orleans and Saigon. He wanted to know how I got along with the people in these places. I told him he would enjoy all of these places and that he would probably reach them all someday.

"Time is on your side," I told him. "After all I have never been to your home state of Montana. Big sky country."

"You will," Dan said.

Dan was a good steady driver. I tried my best to stay awake the last hour of the trip, but the Sandman caught up with me. The next thing I remember was Dan coming to a halt at the ship. He accepted the 20 dollars I handed him then reached in his pocket and handed me ten back. He said they both enjoyed making the trip with me. They would be at the club if I had the time to have a beer with them before the ship sailed.

◆   ◆   ◆

Back aboard ship the next day was routine. Martinjak and some of the rest of us managed to get some more beer. I topped off my supply to carry me through the hot weather that we'd be having for many days to come. After lunch I went ashore and picked up my maroon, tailor-made shoes. They fit like a glove.

Back on the ship, Charlie was comparing notes with K.O. concerning their girlfriends. The sailing board had been set. We would be sailing the next afternoon. After dinner we all made a mad rush down the gangway to have one more fling with the Thai girls. Thailand had proven to be just as popular as Saigon. It was more relaxing in Thailand because we were out of the War Zone and didn't have to worry about running afoul of the curfew. A good time was had by all ashore. Nobody was robbed or rolled on their way to town or back to the ship. I met up with Chon and we had one more lovely evening together. She told me she had several relatives attending Universities in California and Washington. One day she would like to visit them in the States. I encouraged her to keep trying and she might get her wish. At 22, time was definitely on her side. As I left her place the next morning we kissed goodbye and I thought of an old saying I heard from a sailor nearly ten years earlier: "All closed eyes are not asleep and all goodbyes are not gone." I also fantasized about us getting together again in some place other than Sattahip, maybe in San Francisco or Seattle. I shared that thought with her as I handed her 20 dollars.

When reaching the ship I learned that the sailing board had been changed. We would sail the same time the following day. After serving dinner I decided to go to the base club instead of venturing back into town. I caught up with Dan and Bill. They were at a table with two of their Army buddies and several Thai girls. They insisted that I join them. I agreed, but not for long since I had to face an early morning sailing. It was an enjoyable evening drinking and partying with these young people. They were all well behaved in spite of the number of beers they were consuming. I insisted on buying a round for the table. I told Dan and Bill that I would miss them and thanked them again for helping me get to Bangkok. Dan thought it was no big deal and said we might do it again sometime. The girls were smiling and adding so much charm to the party. I ordered another round. The other soldiers at the table asked me about some of the ports I had been to. One of them asked me what we brought to Saigon. I told him I didn't know what was in the cargo hold and couldn't discuss it if I did. Bill thanked me for taking time out to come say so long. Bill took care of the next round. He played a trick on me, ordering me a double bourbon and 7-Up. I could not get it through their heads that I had an early morning getaway ahead of me. Bill reminded me that I could sleep at sea. He also said that they didn't get a chance to associate with American civilians too often in Thailand so it was a special occasion. I was getting a bit high, but the drinks kept coming and the merry-making continued. What saved me was the fact that the club would soon close for the night. When that time came, Dan got me a ride back to the ship. That meant I didn't have to face any snakes crossing the road. I admit I was walking a little wobbly so they insisted on helping me into a Military vehicle and told the driver to see me back aboard. The driver laughed as he told me how lucky I was sailing to so many ports. He was from northern California and had never been off the West Coast before coming to Thailand for Military duty. He said he wished he could trade places with me.

Since he was barely out of his teens, I told him the same thing I told Chon, "Time is on your side." When we reached the ship I convinced him I could walk up the gangway ladder on my own. He still walked up the ladder behind me until I got on the ship. He refused the tip I tried to give him and jokingly told me I could buy him a beer my next trip through; but only if I made it back within two months when he would be ending his tour of duty in Thailand. What a laugh on my part.

I thanked him and he answered, "You're welcome," as he headed back down the ladder.

All the Military longshoremen were busy working on the cargo, making sure we sailed as scheduled. Before going in to bed I noticed that the sailing board now read: "Subic Bay, Philippines at 08:00."

I wrote both Dan and Bill notes of thanks when I returned to the States, but as things happened, we never met again. In later years I made two more visits to Thailand but never saw Chon again either.

15

THE PHILIPPINES

As we sailed out of Sattahip and the Gulf of Siam the crew was really excited about another port where the passwords would be wine, women, and song. Some of the crew failed to remember that they also had their jobs to cover. They let the ladies of the evening become the primary concern. So often this would happen in the last port before returning to the States, especially when the port is like Subic Bay where so many good times are available in such a short period of time.

We were about to enter port in the Philippines; the third "good time" port in a row. The old timers warned that you must let your conscience be your guide. Many of the crewmembers and several officers did not heed that advice. Lucky for them they became wiser by far after the first night ashore. They returned to the ship the next day all hungover after a night on the town with their Filipino sweethearts. They could hardly get through the day. After a verbal reprimand from their respective bosses most of them straightened up and were given another chance.

There were a few who just couldn't, or wouldn't, get the message. They came back to the ship again unable to work without jeopardizing the safety of their fellow crewmembers or themselves. A few of these men worked in the Deck Department and others in the Engine Room. They would be hailed before the Captain and would end up with their names in the log book. At the end of the trip they would be joining the Suitcase Brigade. While most of these men were non-licensed crewmen, it was not unheard of for an officer to be a part of the Brigade. If the offense was not serious enough to warrant a Coast Guard investigation and confiscation of their Seamen documents, many of them would stay ashore for awhile to thaw out and then play the Union Hall and sail out on another ship. This was not a difficult task being that we were in the middle of the Vietnam War.

◆   ◆   ◆

Subic Bay was a sparkling Navy base a little less than one hundred miles away from Manila, the capital of the Philippines. This large complex of sailors, Marines and Military dependents made up what looked like a city within itself. The base was complete with housing, bars, restaurants, cafeterias, movie theatres, and recreation courts. It even had university extensions where Military and civilian personnel could further their college education. It seemed to be the ideal overseas tour of duty for the average Military family. Several times I almost lost my way getting through this huge complex on my way to the gate and into the city of Olongapo.

Magsaysay Boulevard is where most of the action was in Olongapo. There were more girls there than the eyes could see and you could do your thing there with no questions asked. Compared to the action in Saigon and Sattahip, Olongapo outdid them both.

You walked in the door of a bar and some girl might say, "You buy me drink?"

In the meantime she's hanging on like a leach. To make a long story short, everybody who wanted a girl could get one, for a small fee that is. You conducted your business with the girl over drinks and maybe a dance or two. Later you and the girl left the bar and went to her place for the night. In the morning, you had the smarts to get up and return to the ship in time to cover your job. If not, you joined the Suitcase Brigade at the end of the voyage. It's fair to say that not all the Filipino girls are streetwalkers and bar hustlers. There are many Filipinos living outside the naval base in the slums of Olongapo and nearby Subic City who live in poverty but still stick to their family values and the values of their Roman Catholic faith. Many girls grew up decent and married American servicemen who brought them to the States. Filipino men, for many years, joined the U.S. Navy and ended up moving to the States. Many Filipinos worked on the American Military bases such as Subic Bay Naval Base and Clark Air Force Base. They would work on the bases long enough to retire and return to their communities with U.S. Government pensions.

I decided to see some of the community on my own since we would be in port almost a week. I met a thirty-ish woman named Elana my first day in port. She was all too willing to be my tour guide. She was working at the Marine Staff N.C.O. Club on the base. On her night off she took me on a round of the other bars and clubs on Magsaysay Boulevard. We had a ball. Elana spoke better

English than I did. I found many other people I met there also spoke very good English. I guess it was a carryover from Colonial times.

As we made the rounds Elana explained that the two dark-skinned girls across the bar were part Black and part Filipino. I had already figured that out. At another table, an American sailor and his Filipino girlfriend were in what seemed to be a heated argument. They were sitting at a table just across from us. They were finally told by the manager to tone it down or leave. The sailor stormed out of the bar with his girlfriend in hot pursuit. What a scene! Elana said that the sailor, who was stationed on the base, had been caught taking up with another girl behind his girlfriend's back. According to Elana, who knew the girl, it was not the first time she had caught him butterflying.

Most girls will turn vicious on their man if they catch them flying from woman to woman looking for new romances. Then in turn, the girls will do some butterflying of their own when their man is stranded on the base or shipped out on duty. Some girls see it as a chance to make some extra money. After all, business is business.

Elana was my constant companion while at the N.C.O. Club. Since civilians had base privileges there, I would sit with her each night. She would visit with me on her breaks and if she got off early enough, she would take me home with her. I gave her money and purchased gifts for her at the Navy Exchange like name brand perfume. Elana was worth her weight in gold, dollars, or pesos.

The N.C.O. Club was quite lively on Saturday night. There was a big show complete with a band, emcee, and singers. I'd say it was one of the best clubs in Subic Bay. It featured first class entertainment often headed by big name or former big name entertainers with Department of Defense contracts. The Marines, sailors, and entertainers always welcomed us when we came in. The emcee would sometimes announce the name of our ship and ask us to stand and identify ourselves. Such unexpected attention and applause would catch us by surprise. The place was crowded with service personnel, civilians, and some local girls from the city, all out looking for action and a good time. Quite a few of my shipmates would bring their girlfriends from Olongapo in for dinner and dancing or to see the show before returning to their homes with them for a night of fun and relaxation. Really we had it made as long as we covered our shipboard duties. You can't mix too much pleasure with business.

Sixteen years later, in the spring of 1983, I returned to the N.C.O. Club and had the pleasure of meeting the late great LaVerne Baker. Miss Baker was a famous Rock-n-Roll star in the mid-to-late 1950's and now was the head entertainer at the Marine N.C.O. Club with a Department of Defense contract. Those of us on the ship got to become very well acquainted with her. I would go even farther to say we became friends since the ship I was working on at the time stayed in the shipyard in Subic Bay about six weeks. Many of us would go to the club to catch her show before going into Olongapo. LaVerne always treated us as her top dogs. At my request, she sang two old songs from the 50's for me: "I Cried a Tear" and "Shake a Hand." One night I brought her a Soul dinner from the ship. She ate it up. When I learned she wore Estée Lauder perfume, I made a special trip to the Navy Exchange to get her a bottle. I felt so honored to be invited to her table during intermission.

After the overhaul and repair work on the ship was complete, we sailed back to Diego Garcia on station in the Indian Ocean. I stayed in touch with LaVerne Baker for several years. I caught her show again on future trips to the Philippines. She played the same club in 1985, 1987, 1988, and 1989. When I read of her death in 1997 I felt I had lost a friend.

◆   ◆   ◆

Elana wanted to show me around the resort city of Baguio and the capital city of Manila. My duties would not allow it. I had to make do with the few local sites available. With Elana I really had a good time. I wished for a few more days in port, but with the cargo loaded it was time to move on. Some of the crew in the Deck and Engine Departments got carried away. Four of them would be brought before Captain Schraeder. Their names would be entered in the log book and they would be fired upon reaching Seattle. Martinjak for some reason decided to quench his thirst with San Miguel beer using rum as a chaser. Upon returning to the ship the next morning, he went to bed instead of doing his duties in the Engine Room. For this, he earned the distinction of being the only officer to join the Suitcase Brigade. It was all quiet in the Steward Department, even from Jesse.

The night before sailing Juan threw us a party at one of the clubs in Olongapo. It was a nice catered affair. We met some of his relatives still living in the Philippines. Elana came along as my guest. All the crew who showed up brought a girl along. The place was loaded with lovely girls so no one missed out. Juan and some of his relatives fixed all of the food. I made a pig of myself on the pork adobe, noodles, and beer. What a party! On Monday morning the sailing board left no doubt in my mind that this voyage was almost over. It read: "Seattle, Washington."

I enjoyed my visit to the Philippines. We were able to walk the streets of Olongapo and Subic City without incident. No reports of attacks, muggings, or any other kinds of assaults. I walked dark streets and alleys at night and never had anyone bother me. I can't even do that in my hometown back in the States. In the late 1960's Ferdinand Marcos was running the show in the Philippines with his fair lady Imelda at his side. He kept things under control by ruling with an iron hand. The agreements on the Military bases remained intact. Sad to say by the time I returned to the Philippines in the 1980's tragedy and violence had begun to rise and Americans were not immune.

As we sailed out of Subic Bay and away from the late April heat of the tropics, I reminisced about what a wonderful experience these two voyages had been for me. I met complete strangers who would become long lasting friends. People I met from other cultures, though poor and downtrodden, taught me how to really live.

I had picked up the *Stars and Stripes* from the Navy Exchange and would read it after work. For the next two weeks at sea we swapped stories of our voyage until we finally reached Pier 91 in Seattle.

Charlie's wife, Emma threw a big homecoming party for the crew at their home on Yesler Way. Everyone who wasn't on duty made it for the food, drink, and to meet some of the many people there. It was a time for celebration. Jesse and the entire Steward Department, and several officers, including Martinjak, were there. The next day Jesse and Martinjak would get their payoffs and by afternoon be on the same flight traveling east. Martinjak's drinking buddy Jim Long was also at the party. He managed not mix too much business with pleasure and would be able to make another trip. Since both Charlie and Bruce were staying for another trip, I told Charlie to sleep in and I would cover his duties onboard the ship the next morning. My offer pleased both Charlie and his wife. K.O. told me he would also be staying for another voyage. I wasn't too surprised because I knew the *Marine Charger* was headed back to Southeast Asia. After five days in Seattle, I decided to stay on for another voyage as well. We would be headed along the coast to San Francisco and then back across the Pacific Ocean. Juan, Ken, Dale, Larry, and Jake could hardly wait. To be truthful all of us in the Steward Department were excited.

In the Deck Department, Bob the Bos'n was happy to know that the majority of his ABs and Ordinary Seamen were staying on except of course those who had gotten themselves put in the Suitcase Brigade. Even these men would return to the sea after a few weeks layoff. None of their offenses were serious enough to have their Seamen documents taken away by the Coast Guard. They would have little trouble finding a position aboard a ship during this phase of the Vietnam War.

EPILOGUE

When Jesse left the ship that spring afternoon in Seattle, we both swore we would stay in touch. We pledged this again at Charlie's party that night. In spite of Jesse's drunken behavior we would always remain friends. He told me some personal things about his wife that he would rather the rest of the crew didn't know and I kept it in strict confidence. His replacement on the next voyage and I were not close friends. In letters I wrote to Jesse during this first voyage apart, I told him how much he was missed especially his skill as a cook and a baker. He wrote to me about a trip he and Juhl had taken to Louisiana, and how much they enjoyed themselves. Jesse asked me to call him at the end of the voyage. I did just that in late August 1967. What I learned made me very sad. Jesse's lovely wife, Juhl was up to the same games she played in Capetown. She picked up rich White men and got paid big money for her sexual favors. Juhl had come a long way from her humble surroundings in Capetown. The Natives and "Coloreds" there were relegated to the lower rung of the ladder by the White establishment. Jesse had brought her away from all that by marrying her and arranging for her to come to America and to a better life. Juhl had no reason to continue soliciting men anymore. Jesse had given her a nice home in an upper-middle class neighborhood in Hempstead and sent her generous allotments when he was away at sea. You would think she had it made but sometimes old habits die hard. Juhl didn't realize how different Capetown was from New York. In Capetown, she would ply her trade at first class hotels where she met wealthy men among the registered guests or at house parties like the one she was working when she met Jesse.

In New York, she made contacts. She would travel into the city from Hempstead two or three times a week then return to her safe haven on Long Island. This plan worked for awhile until one hot summer evening in midtown Manhattan when she solicited a plain-clothes police officer and was busted on the spot. Juhlene DeGroot Davis had met her Waterloo. She played a foolish game and lost everything. She was found guilty in court and deported back to South Africa. Jesse was devastated. I told him how sorry I was about his tragic misfortune and we continued to keep in touch during the whole ordeal. Jesse was too ashamed to bare his soul so he simply told friends and relatives that he and Juhl had broken up. Jesse was a forgiving man and deep in his heart he still loved Juhl in spite of her infidelity. He needed to talk things over with Juhl, but knew if he told his friends about his plans they would try to talk him out of it. His family would try to persuade him to let her go. Just as I knew Jesse, I knew he would have it his own way. He left his New York home under the care of a cousin and flew to New Orleans. He registered at the Union Hall and only had to wait two days before he was boarding a ship as Second Cook and sailing to South Africa in search of his lost Juhl.

◆   ◆   ◆

I applied to San Francisco State College in the late 1960's but was denied admission because of a low grade point average. I made up the deficiency through summer sessions and was finally admitted in 1971. I graduated with a Bachelor of Arts degree in History in June 1972. I was in the last commencement ceremony that Dr. Hayakawa presided over at San Francisco State. He joked about always wanting to be president of a university, which San Francisco State became that year.

When I returned to Bayonne, New Jersey in early November 1976 I had dinner at my older sister's apartment then went out on the town losing myself again in New York's Harlem. I took the next afternoon off, determined to renew old acquaintances. I wanted to brace myself so I stopped at a bar just outside the gate on East 32nd Street. I remembered this bar from more than two decades earlier. It was a stop off for sailors going between the base and their ships. This bar was run by a man called Ziggy and his mother, referred to by everyone as "Mom." Mom spoke with what sounded like a Polish accent. They kept order in a firm sort of way, both demanding and getting respect from bar patrons, civilians, and sailors alike.

But that was some 23 years ago. I enquired of one of the older patrons and learned that both Mom and Ziggy had passed on. I finished my beer and went up the street to Broadway. It seemed like everything I was looking for was just around some other corner like an elusive dream. I stopped in another bar. I asked the young bartender if he was in any way acquainted with Our Lady of Assumption Church. With a surprised look on his face he told me he was a member. I asked him about Father D and he told me that the Reverend had died a few years past.

"I'm sorry," was my reply, as I took my third blow in less than an hour.

Since there were few customers in the bar at the time, the bartender talked at length about Father D. He told me how Father D had been striving and working hard for the betterment of the church just before his death. I told him about not having seen him in 21 years. Had I not missed the opportunity in 1966 we could have met once more before the end. As I left I thanked him for his hospitality and information then turned and walked down the street toward Hudson Boulevard, now renamed Kennedy Boulevard. Once on the boulevard I flipped a mental coin. Should I walk across to the church or board a bus to New York and attend a movie in Times Square. The latter choice won out. When a bus rolled up in less than 20 minutes, I climbed aboard. During the bus ride to Times Square nostalgia gave way to sadness. Before reaching New York's port authority I had pulled myself together and done some sober thinking. Many years had passed since Father D and his lay assistants had taken me into their community. They had become my spiritual advisors as I entered my new-found faith. Some gave me such things as medals and statues at confirmation time. Over the years, I felt like I let them down. By indulging in too much worldly behavior, I got out of touch. In hindsight I could have squeezed in some time to renew old friendships and acquaintances during many visits to New York and Philadelphia over the years. As for this visit, I think I was justified not to stop by the church or the rectory to look up anyone who might still be around. I considered myself not worthy to go back under their roof.

◆   ◆   ◆

By the time I traveled to Australia again it was 1978. They had begun to open their doors to Asians and people of African descent. In the mid-1970's many Vietnamese entered Australia seeking refuge from their war torn country. Less known African American entertainers and sports figures moved there as well, usually settling in the larger cities.

The next time Judy and I met she had been married for four years to a fellow New Zealander. They had a two year old daughter. Judy and I had a platonic meeting in the Cross at a restaurant just across the street from *The Greenroom* where we first met. Her husband had a high paying job on the Sydney waterfront and insisted that she not work until their daughter grew older. Judy's husband Allan had bought them a home in Balmain, a distance away from the Cross. She introduced me to her daughter over dinner. She was named after Judy's best friend and roommate, Heather. The original Heather and her boyfriend George got married several years earlier.

I offered her some assistance for old time's sake, but she politely declined saying she was alright. We parted company for the last time, on a very friendly note.

I also caught up with my friends Ian and Jennifer in suburban Brisbane on that particular voyage to Australia. They had bought a new and larger home in the same old community. I could see why: they had added three children to their family. Jennifer was taking over full-time responsibility as a mother, scaling down her hours at the bank. On the other hand, Ian was in the process of taking over his parents' business because they were on the verge of retirement. The years had been kind to them.

When I returned to New Orleans, a decade after my first visit, I was happy to see that Adrian had finally found happiness with a man she married five years earlier. Since remarrying, she had a four year old daughter. Her son was then in middle school. She had a part-time office job. For old time's sake, we had dinner and drinks, but in a strictly platonic sense. We both understood.

Young Breaux finished college at Dillard. He got married to the same girl he wanted me to meet. Not only did I meet her, they had me come to their home for dinner where I pigged on some good Creole cooking. Breaux was an instructor in social studies at one of the local high schools. His wife Janice was a substitute teacher. They were proud parents of a five year old daughter and a four year old son. Breaux got his wish to travel the world. He had done so in an Army hitch, serving a tour of duty in Germany. While there, he took leave to England and France. I was happy to see that my earlier advice to him paid off: "Get the education first and travel the world later."

Adrian's coworkers, Larry and Dottie, were still working at the Cafeteria. Some of their children had grown up. They were both happy to see me. I was also happy to see that Larry was still the responsible family man and Dottie had toned down on drinking.

I kept in touch with some of my shipmates from the *Marine Charger* over the years. Some others I ran into in various shipping halls in later years. Sully and Martinjak went back into retirement five years after our two voyages together. We fell out of touch after ten years. If they still live they would be very old men. Bob Harris, the Bos'n, kept sailing until 1998, when he retired to Hayward, California with his wife and dog.

Bruce Williams, the Chief Steward, retired in 1975 to New Jersey. He and his wife eventually moved back to their roots in Texas where, as far as I know, they still live today.

Kevin "K.O." O'Keefe gave up shipping after the Vietnam War. He and several other guys opened up a fancy bar and restaurant in Boston. The last time I heard from him, he and his wife and family were getting along quiet well. Apparently he had given up his fancy for Asian women.

My fellow Messman Charlie retired to Seattle in 1974 at the age of 74. We kept in touch until he passed on 14 years later. Until the end, he was an immaculate dresser, with a closet full of clothes of the latest style. The same went for his wife Emma. Not only did they rub shoulders with Seattle's elite, they would fly to New York and San Francisco at least once a year to visit with friends and relatives. They would wine and dine in exclusive clubs and restaurants. His widow, Emma, still lives in Seattle with their granddaughter. She enjoys good health even while approaching her late 90's.

Betty and I never married but we remain partners in life to this day.

On both voyages on the *Marine Charger* I built long lasting friendships with my fellow shipmates as well as people I met in our ports of call. Many of these people I never saw again, but they left me with precious memories that will last a life time.

The aforementioned people who I did get to see again—in most cases—had half grown or fully grown children. Seeing this made me realize one thing. Time had passed me by.

978-0-595-36587-6
0-595-36587-6